FOR THE OLDER BEGINNER

ACCELERATED
PIANO
Adventures® *by Nancy and Randall Faber*

W9-AQS-678

Student's Name ————————————————
Starting Date ————————————————
Teacher's Name ————————————————
Teacher's Phone Number ————————————————

FABER
PIANO ADVENTURES®
3042 Creek Drive
Ann Arbor, Michigan 48108

CONTENTS

The student may wish to put a ✔ or date in the blank as each piece is completed.

TREBLE SPACE NOTES: F-A-C-E

TREBLE C PENTASCALE: TREBLE C D E F G

INTERVALS: 4TH AND 5TH

SHARPS AND FLATS

I AND V[7] CHORDS

THREE G PENTASCALES

Getting to Know You

1. What type of piano do you have in your home? *(circle)*

upright   *grand*   *digital keyboard*

2. Have you had music classes at school? _____

3. Do you play any other musical instrument(s)? _____

If so, write them here: _____

4. Does anyone in your family play a musical instrument(s)? _____

If so, write them here:_____

_____

5. Circle any music symbols that you know. Define each for your teacher.

6. Can you play any tunes "by ear" on the piano? _____

If so, play them for your teacher.

7. Have you ever made up (composed) your own music on the piano? _____

8. What are your favorite types of music?

(blues, classical, country, gospel, jazz, pop, rap, rock, etc.)

Write them here: _____

9. Have you ever been to a band, choir, or orchestra concert? _____

(Tell your teacher something you liked about it.)

10. Are there any songs or pieces you would especially like to learn as you take piano lessons? Write the titles below.

_____   _____

_____   _____

Sitting at the Piano

1. Distance Check

- Sit straight and tall on the front half of the bench.

- With your arms straight, **your knuckles should reach the fallboard**. (If you have to lean, move the bench forward or backward.)

Sit on the front half of the bench.

feet flat on the floor

2. Seating Height Check

- With shoulders relaxed, place your hands on the keys.

- **Your forearms should be level with the keyboard.** Adjust your seating height up or down as needed.

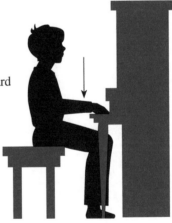

forearms level with the keyboard

3. Posture Check

- Take a deep breath and let it out.

- Are you sitting tall, yet with **shoulders down and relaxed**?

shoulders relaxed

This is your position for playing the piano.

Finger Numbers

Each finger is given a number—1, 2, 3, 4, or 5.

- Wiggle both finger **1's**, finger **2's**, finger **3's**, finger **4's**, and finger **5's**.

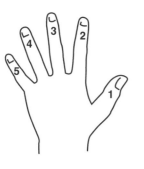

L.H.
stands for
Left Hand

R.H.
stands for
Right Hand

*Keep your fingernails
trimmed so you can easily
play on your fingertips.*

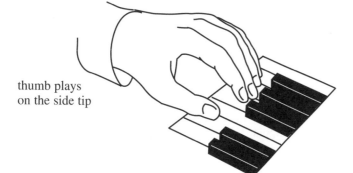

rounded hand position

thumb plays
on the side tip

Hand Position

- Let your arms hang loosely at your sides.
  Notice the **natural curve** of your fingers.

- Now gently place your hands on the keys.

  It is important to keep a relaxed, curved hand
  position as you play the piano.

Finger Drill on the Keyboard

With a **rounded hand position** and **firm fingertips**:

1. Choose any white key and play it with RIGHT HAND finger 1, then 2, then 3, then 4, then 5.
   (Hint: Play the thumb on the *side tip*.)

2. Choose any white key and play it with RIGHT HAND finger 5, then 4, then 3, then 2, then 1.

3. Choose any white key and play it with LEFT HAND finger 1, then 2, then 3, then 4, then 5.

4. Choose any white key and play it with LEFT HAND finger 5, then 4, then 3, then 2, then 1.

FF1205

High and Low on the Keyboard

The piano KEYBOARD has white keys and black keys.

Notice the black keys are in groups of **two's** and **three's**.

ow 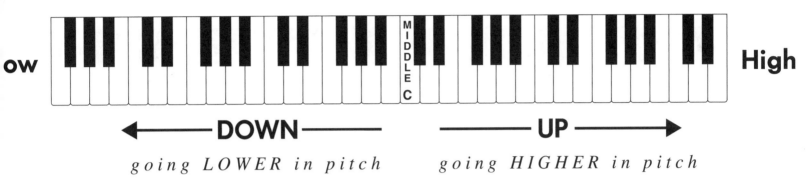 High

← DOWN ———— UP →

going LOWER in pitch   *going HIGHER in pitch*

Teacher: Demonstrate the exercises below for the student.

Wind Chimes for Right Hand

With your right foot, hold the damper pedal down (the pedal on the right).

- Begin and end in the MIDDLE of the keyboard.

- Play the 2-black-key groups going UP, then back DOWN the keyboard (higher, then lower). Use R.H. fingers 2 and 3.

- Play *forte* (loudly).

> *forte* (pronounced FOR-tay) is the Italian word for loud.
>
> *f* is the abbreviation for *forte*.

Wind Chimes for Left Hand

Hold the damper pedal down.

- Begin and end in the MIDDLE of the keyboard.

- Play the 2-black-key groups going DOWN, then back UP the keyboard (lower, then higher). Use L.H. fingers 2 and 3.

- Play *piano* (softly).

> *piano* is the Italian word for soft.
>
> *p* is the abbreviation for *piano*.

DISCOVERY

Play *Wind Chimes* using fingers 2-3-4 on the **3-black-key** groups.

The Music Alphabet

Each white key has a name from the music alphabet: **A B C D E F G**.

Play and name aloud the white keys from *lowest* to *highest*.
(Use L.H. finger 3 for lower notes; R.H. finger 3 for higher notes.)

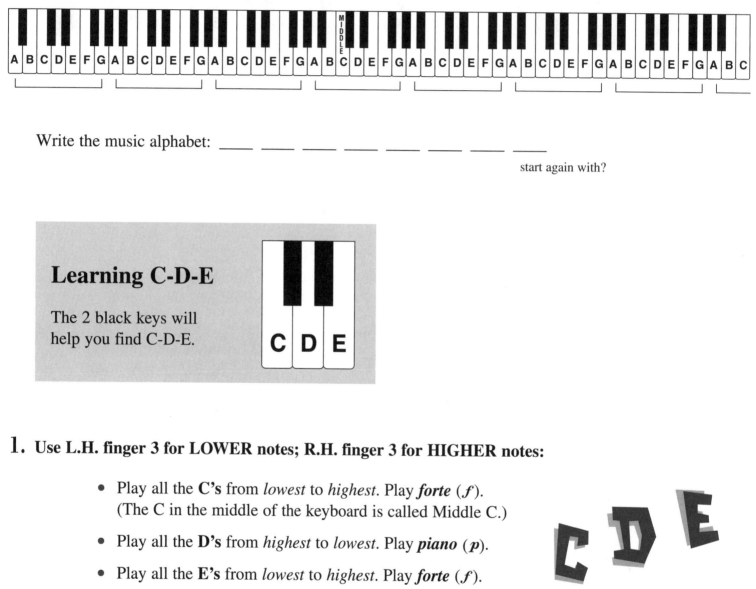

Write the music alphabet: ____ ____ ____ ____ ____ ____ ____ ____

start again with?

Learning C-D-E

The 2 black keys will
help you find C-D-E.

C D E

1. **Use L.H. finger 3 for LOWER notes; R.H. finger 3 for HIGHER notes:**

   - Play all the **C's** from *lowest* to *highest*. Play *forte* (*f*).
     (The C in the middle of the keyboard is called Middle C.)

   - Play all the **D's** from *highest* to *lowest*. Play *piano* (*p*).

   - Play all the **E's** from *lowest* to *highest*. Play *forte* (*f*).

2. With the damper pedal down, play **C and E together** using R.H. fingers 1 and 3.
   Begin in the MIDDLE of the keyboard and play C and E *higher* and *higher*. Play *piano* (*p*).

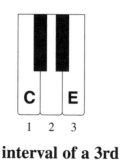

interval of a 3rd

An **interval** is the distance between two keys.
From C to E is the interval of a **third (3rd)**.

FF120

Learning F-G-A-B

The 3 black keys will
help you find F-G-A-B.

3. Use L.H. finger 3 for LOWER notes; R.H. finger 3 for HIGHER notes:

- Play all the **F's** from *lowest* to *highest*. Play *forte* (*f*).

- Play all the **G's** from *highest* to *lowest*. Play *piano* (*p*).

- Play all the **A's** from *lowest* to *highest*. Play *forte* (*f*).

- Play all the **B's** from *highest* to *lowest*. Play *piano* (*p*).

4. With the damper pedal down, play **F and A together** using L.H. fingers 1 and 3.
Begin in the MIDDLE of the keyboard and play F and A *lower* and *lower*. Play *piano* (*p*).

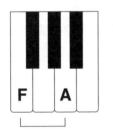

Remember, this **interval** is a **3rd**.

5. With the damper pedal down, play **G and B together** using R.H. fingers 2 and 4.
Begin in the MIDDLE of the keyboard and play G and B *higher* and *higher*. Play *forte* (*f*).

What interval are you playing? _____

D I S C O V E R Y
Close your eyes and play any white key. Open your eyes and name the key.

Rhythm

Music has long and short sounds. We count the long and short sounds with a **steady beat** (or pulse). This creates RHYTHM.

Directions:

1. Clap or tap the "Rhythm Flag" from top to bottom, counting aloud.
   Feel a steady beat.

2. Choose any white key and play the notes in the "Rhythm Flag" from top to bottom, then bottom to top. (Your teacher will demonstrate.)
   Feel a steady beat as you count and play.

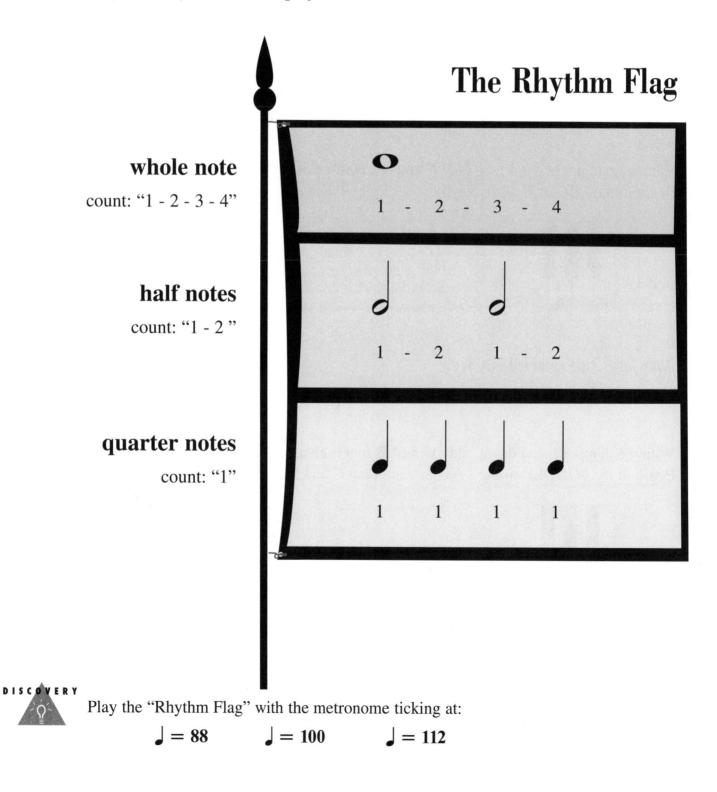

The Rhythm Flag

whole note

count: "1 - 2 - 3 - 4"

1 - 2 - 3 - 4

half notes

count: "1 - 2 "

1 - 2   1 - 2

quarter notes

count: "1"

1   1   1   1

DISCOVERY

Play the "Rhythm Flag" with the metronome ticking at:

♩ = 88   ♩ = 100   ♩ = 112

FF120

The Measure

Beats are grouped into measures.
Each measure has the same number of beats.

Bar lines divide the music into measures.
- How many measures are in the piece below?

Warm-up for R.H.

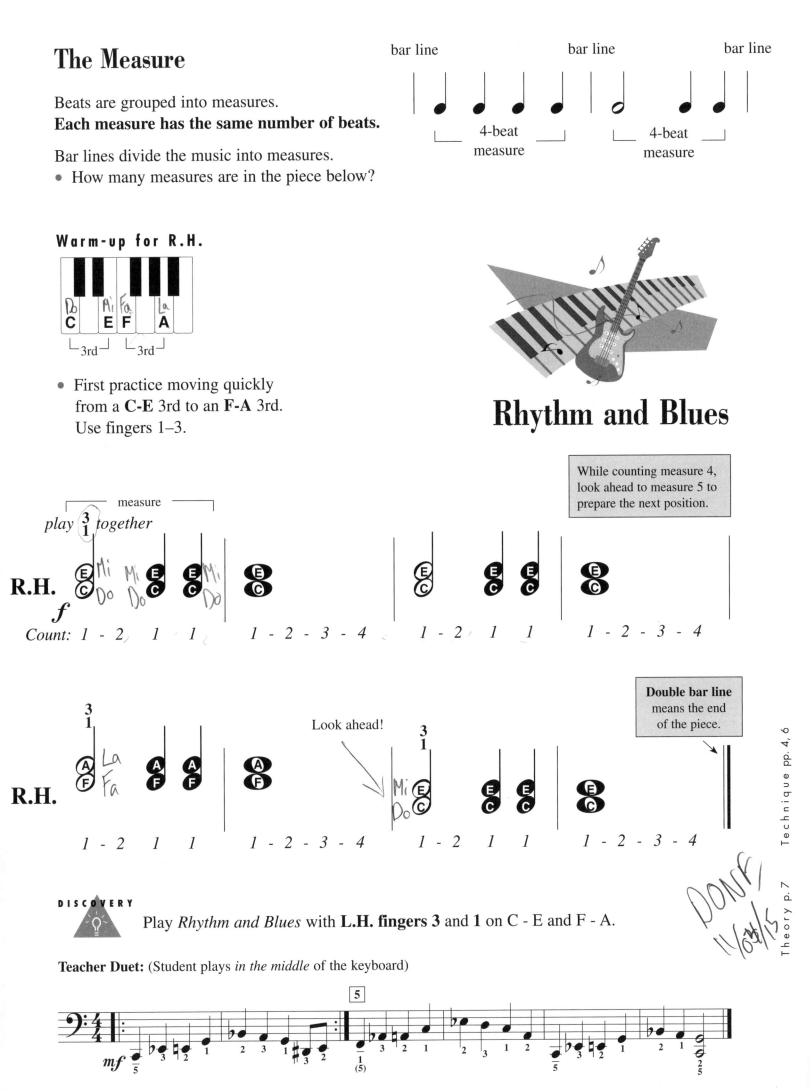

- First practice moving quickly from a **C-E** 3rd to an **F-A** 3rd. Use fingers 1–3.

Rhythm and Blues

While counting measure 4, look ahead to measure 5 to prepare the next position.

play together

R.H.

f

Count: *1 - 2   1   1   1 - 2 - 3 - 4   1 - 2   1   1   1 - 2 - 3 - 4*

Double bar line means the end of the piece.

R.H.

Look ahead!

1 - 2   1   1   1 - 2 - 3 - 4   1 - 2   1   1   1 - 2 - 3 - 4

DISCOVERY

Play *Rhythm and Blues* with **L.H. fingers 3** and **1** on C - E and F - A.

Teacher Duet: (Student plays *in the middle* of the keyboard)

Theory p.7   Technique pp. 4, 6

Seconds (2nds)

Remember, an *interval* is the distance between two keys.

The interval of a **2nd** (or **step**) moves up or down to the:

next KEY — next LETTER NAME — next FINGER

Ex. **C - D**

(handwritten right margin:) f = forte (loud) p = piano (quiet)

The word scale comes from the Latin word *scala*, meaning "ladder." The notes of a scale move up and down by **2nds** (steps). Penta means "five." A *pentascale* is a 5-note scale.

Practice Suggestions:

1. Play *in the middle* of the keyboard, saying the letter names aloud. Keep the quarter notes steady.

2. Play in different C Pentascales daily.

C Pentascale

L.H.   R.H.

Do Re Mi Fa Sol   Do Re Mi Fa Sol
C D E F G   C D E F G
5 4 3 2 1   1 2 3 4 5

Exploring Seconds

R.H.

1 2 3 4 5 4 3 2 1 2 3 4 5
Do C / Re D / Mi E / Fa F / Sol G / Fa F / Mi E / Re D / Do C / Re D / Mi E / Fa F / Sol Sol Sol G G G

Step- ping up and step- ping down, I'm play- ing quar- ters stead- i- ly.

f - p on repeat

L.H.

Sec- onds down and sec- onds up, I'm play- ing sec- onds eas- i- ly.

Sol G / Fa F / Mi E / Re D / Do C / Re D / Mi E / Fa F / Sol G / Fa F / Mi E / Re D / Do C / Do C / Do C
1 2 3 4 5 4 3 2 1 2 3 4 5

(handwritten:) 1st time f 2nd time p

Repeat sign
These dots mean to go back to the beginning and play once again.

Technique pp. 4, 7

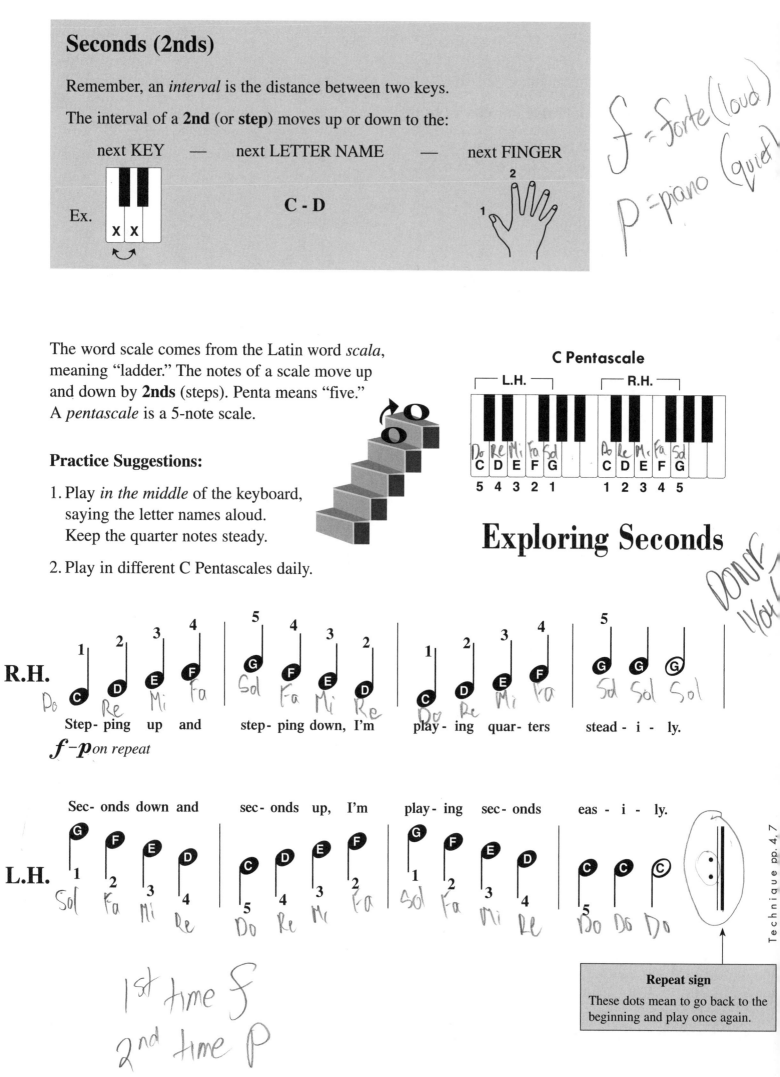

FF1205

Thirds (3rds)

The interval of a **3rd** (or **skip**):

skips a KEY — skips a LETTER NAME — skips a FINGER

Ex.

C - E

[handwritten: ① counts ② note names solfège right left]

[handwritten: octave = 8 notes]

The following piece moves up and down by **3rds** in the C Pentascale.

Practice Suggestions:

1. First clap or tap the rhythm while counting aloud.

2. Play *in the middle* of the keyboard, saying the letter names aloud. Keep the quarter notes steady.

3. Play in different C Pentascales daily.

C Pentascale

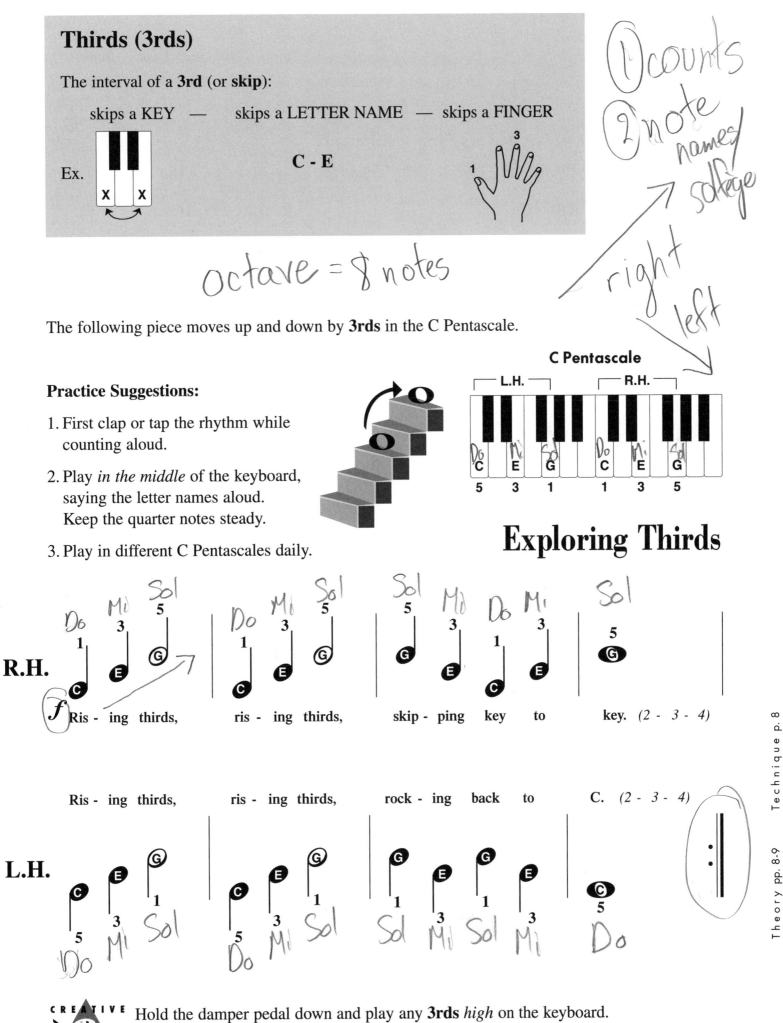

Exploring Thirds

R.H. *f* Ris - ing thirds, ris - ing thirds, skip - ping key to key. *(2 - 3 - 4)*

Ris - ing thirds, ris - ing thirds, rock - ing back to C. *(2 - 3 - 4)*

L.H.

CREATIVE Hold the damper pedal down and play any **3rds** *high* on the keyboard. *Listen* to the sound of 3rds.

Theory pp. 8-9 Technique p. 8

The Staff

Music is written on a staff. A staff has **5** lines and **4** spaces.

Notes are written **on the line**s or **in the spaces** of the staff.

5 Line Notes **4 Space Notes**

- On the staffs below (also called staves), identify each note as a *line* or *space* note.

Middle Do

Bass Clef and Treble Clef

In piano music we use 2 staffs (staves). Together we call them the **GRAND STAFF**.

The **bass clef** shows notes BELOW Middle C. (Bass means *low* sounds.)

- Play Middle C and all the white keys *going down* to the low A shown.

The **treble clef** shows notes ABOVE Middle C. (Treble means *high* sounds.)

- Play Middle C and all the white keys *going up* to the high G shown.

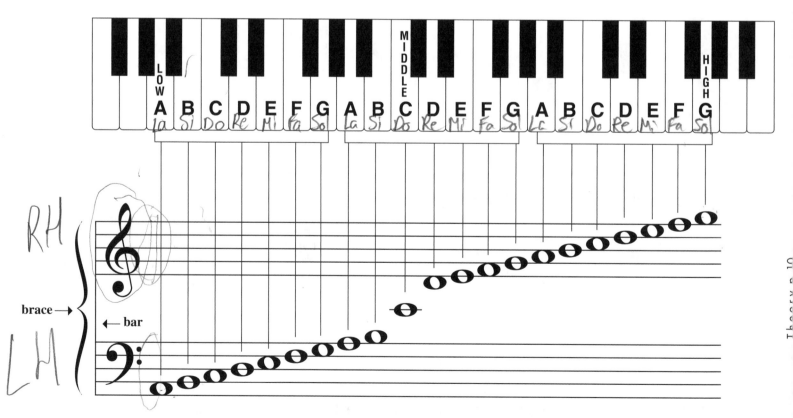

As notes on the staff move from a **space** to the next **line** to the next **space**, etc., they move by **2nds** (steps) on the keyboard. (See page 12.)

14

The **time signature** is written at the beginning of the music.

It indicates the number of beats in each measure.

> **4** = 4 beats in each measure ("1-2-3-4")
> **4** = The quarter note ♩ receives one beat.

This exercise uses only finger 3's.

- First play saying the **letter names**.
  (Begin two A's below middle C.)

- Then play counting aloud, **"1-2-3-4."**
  Accent (play louder) beat 1 of each measure.
  This is an **accent mark**: >

4-Beat Alphabet

> **3** = 3 beats in each measure ("1-2-3")
> **4** = The quarter note ♩ receives one beat.

- Now play feeling **3 beats** per measure.
  Count aloud, **"1-2-3."** Accent beat 1 of each measure.

3-Beat Alphabet

Theory p. 11

Learning Middle C

Middle C is written on a short line (ledger line) between the treble and bass staves.

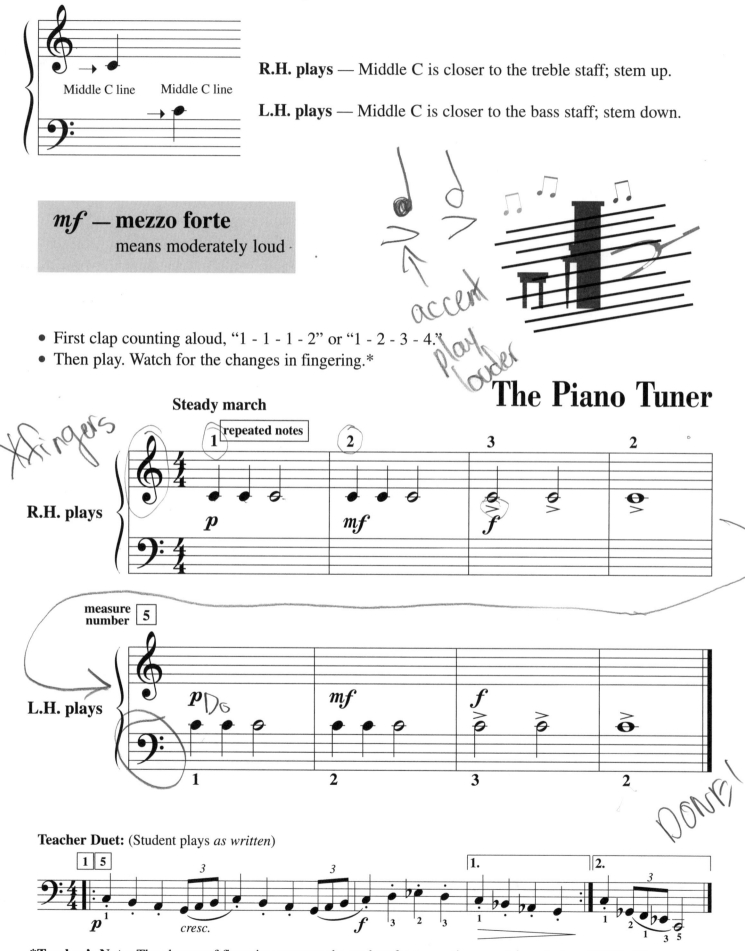

R.H. plays — Middle C is closer to the treble staff; stem up.

L.H. plays — Middle C is closer to the bass staff; stem down.

mf — **mezzo forte**

means moderately loud

- First clap counting aloud, "1 - 1 - 1 - 2" or "1 - 2 - 3 - 4."
- Then play. Watch for the changes in fingering.*

The Piano Tuner

Steady march

R.H. plays

L.H. plays

Teacher Duet: (Student plays *as written*)

*Teacher's Note:** The change of fingering prevents the student from equating a certain note (e.g. Middle C) with a specific finger (e.g. thumb).

16

Learning Treble Clef G

- Find the G five keys above Middle C. This is called **Treble Clef G**.

Do   Sol

Hand Shape Exercise

- With R.H. fingers 1 and 5, play back and forth between Middle C and Treble Clef G. (This is the interval of a 5th.)

- Is **Treble Clef G** written on line 1, 2, 3, 4, or 5? *(circle)*

The treble clef is also called the **G clef** because it circles around the **G line** on the staff. The treble clef came from the old letter G shown below.

G-line

① notes
② counts / rhythm
③ dynamics

Melody on C and G

together

1 *on* Do?   5 *on* Sol?

mf C and G song, Play this C and G song. *(2 - 3 - 4)*

In the tre - ble they be - long. *p*

p = quiet

DISCOVERY Play this piece **hands together**. L.H. plays in a *lower* C Pentascale with fingers 5 and 1. (The letter names stay the same, but the finger numbers will be different.)

DONE

Teacher Duet: (Student plays *as written*)

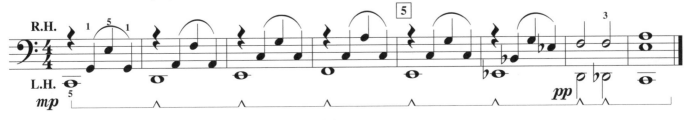

R.H. *mp*   L.H. *pp*

About the Damper Pedal

The **damper pedal** is the pedal on the right.
It lifts the *dampers* (felts) off the strings
which lets the sound continue to ring.

Pedal mark:

Pedal   *hold it down*   Pedal
DOWN   UP

**Use your right foot for the damper pedal.
Keep your heel on the floor.**

- Which R.H. finger now plays **Treble Clef G**?

Fife and Drum

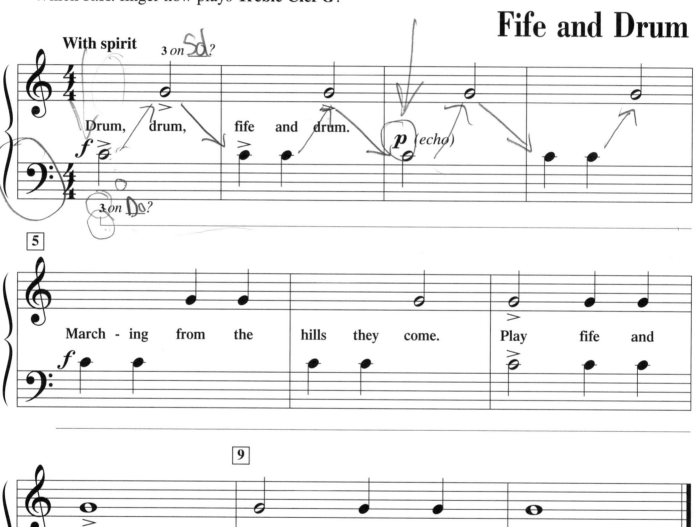

With spirit

Drum, drum, fife and drum. *p* (echo)

Marching from the hills they come. Play fife and

drum! Play fife and drum!

Teacher Duet: (Student plays *as written*)

8va throughout

mf-p on repeat   *mf*   *pp*

18

Theory p.13   Technique p.10

Learning Bass Clef F_a

- Find the F five keys below Middle C.
  This is called **Bass Clef F**.

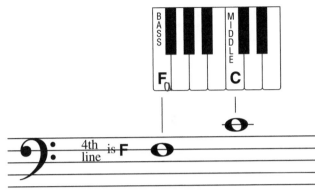

Hand Shape Exercise

- With L.H. fingers 1 and 5, play back and forth between Middle C and Bass Clef F.
  Can you name this interval? _____ (See p. 17)

- Is **Bass Clef F** written on line 1, 2, 3, 4, or 5? *(circle)*

The bass clef is also called the **F clef** because the dots point out the **F line** on the staff. The bass clef came from the old letter F shown below.

Finger Challenge: Play **Bass Clef F** with L.H. finger 5, then 4, then 3. Which finger plays **Bass Clef F** in *My Invention*?

My Invention

Like a machine

My in-ven-tion   is worth men-tion,   if you saw it   you would know.

mf

1 on Do? 5d
3 on Fa?

5

It's fan-tas-tic   and bom-bas-tic   and what's more it   e-ven glows!

D I S C O V E R Y With a highlighter or pencil, trace the bass clef **F line** for the first measure. Your teacher may have you trace the 𝄞 G line and 𝄢 F line for many pieces in the book.

Teacher Duet: (Student plays *as written*)

1 5   *8va throughout*
mp

Guide Notes

Middle C, Treble Clef G, and **Bass Clef F** are the three notes you have learned. These notes will "guide" you as you learn new notes on the staff.

• Name, then play these notes.

Reading 2nds (Steps) with D-E-F

Learn the three notes that are between Guide Notes **Middle C** and **Treble Clef G**.

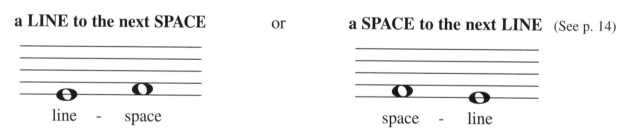

Do   Re   Mi   Fa   Sol

• Play and say: | C | D   E   F | G |
• Play and say: line - space - line - space - line

On the staff, the **interval of a 2nd (step)** is from:

a LINE to the next SPACE   or   **a SPACE to the next LINE**   (See p. 14)

line - space   space - line

• Look at the *noteheads* and circle **UP a 2nd** or **DOWN a 2nd** for each example below.
• Then play each on the piano.

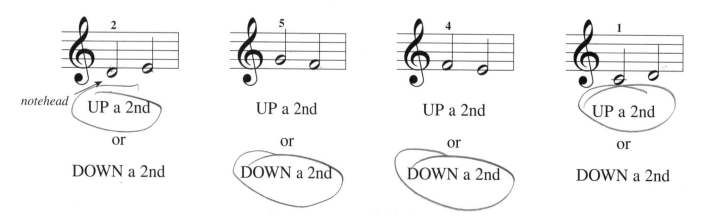

notehead

(UP a 2nd)   UP a 2nd   UP a 2nd   (UP a 2nd)

or   or   or   or

DOWN a 2nd   (DOWN a 2nd)   (DOWN a 2nd)   DOWN a 2nd

Theory p. 14

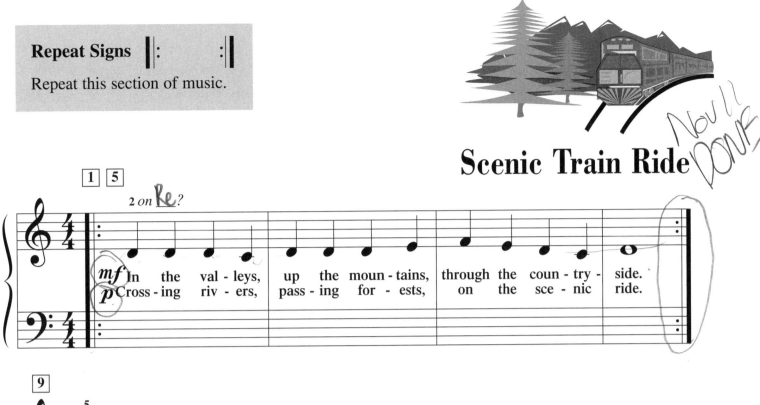

Repeat Signs 𝄆 𝄇

Repeat this section of music.

Scenic Train Ride

Nov 11 DONE

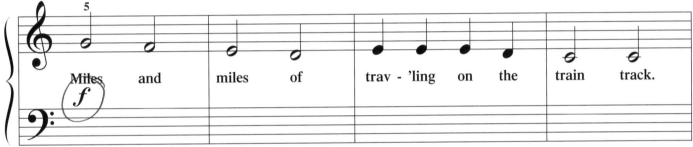

1 5
2 on Re?

mf **In** the val - leys, up the moun - tains, through the coun - try - side.
p **Cross** - ing riv - ers, pass - ing for - ests, on the sce - nic ride.

9
5

Miles and miles of trav - 'ling on the train track.
f

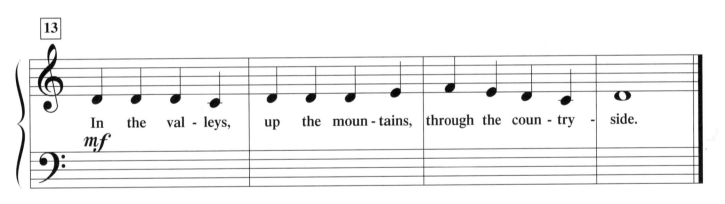

13

In the val - leys, up the moun - tains, through the coun - try - side.
mf

 DISCOVERY Explore playing a **low D-A 5th** with your L.H. at the beginning of the first and last lines of music. Your teacher will help you.

Teacher Duet: (Student plays *1 octave higher*)

1 5 13
R.H.

L.H.
mp–p on repeat

9

mf

1.

2. 3.
Fine

D.C. al Fine

Reading Changes in Direction

The trick to reading 2nds is watching for a **change in direction** (up or down).
Keep your eyes focused on the *noteheads*.

Nov #18

The arrows below show the **up**, **down**, or **repeated** movement of the notes.

Example:

1. Play:

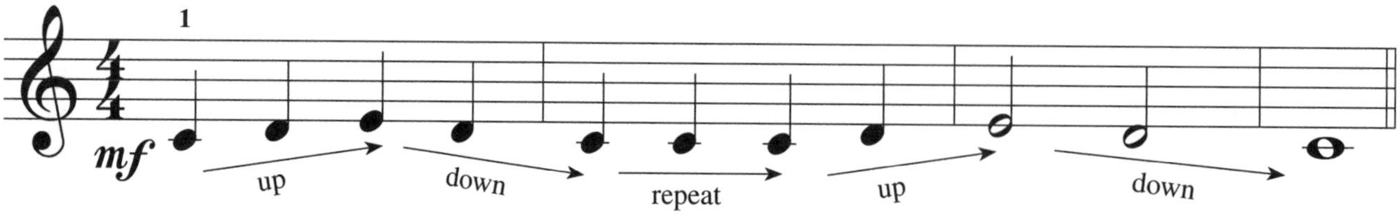

mf up → down → repeat → up → down →

• Draw arrows to show the **up**, **down**, or **repeated** movement of the notes.

2. Play:

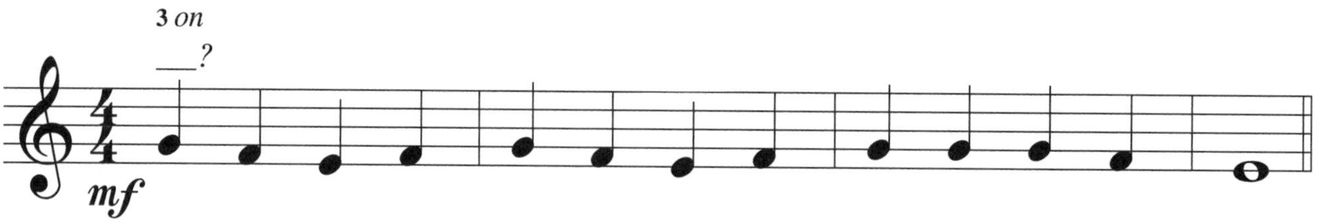

3 on ___?

mf

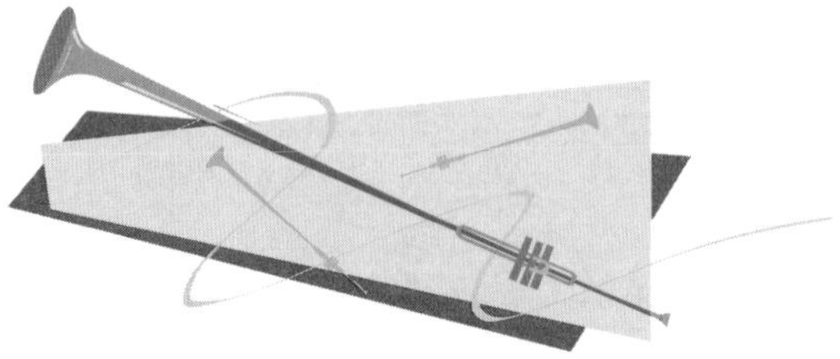

Learn and play this piece by:

• reading **2nds** up and down
• recognizing note names C-D-E-F-G

Roman Trumpets

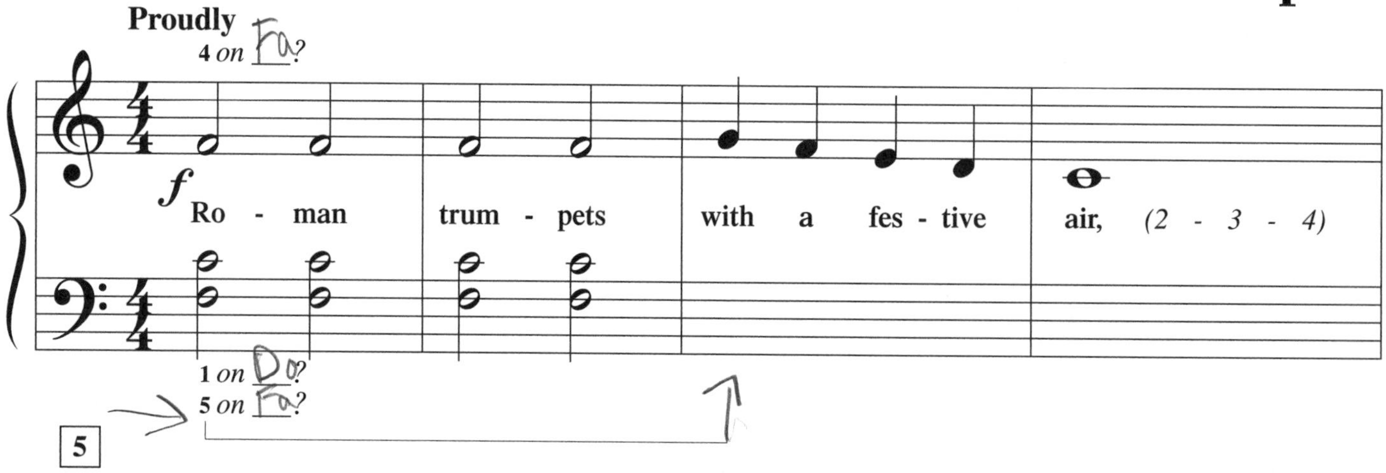

Proudly
4 on Fa?

f Ro - man trum - pets with a fes - tive air, *(2 - 3 - 4)*

1 on Do?
5 on Fa?

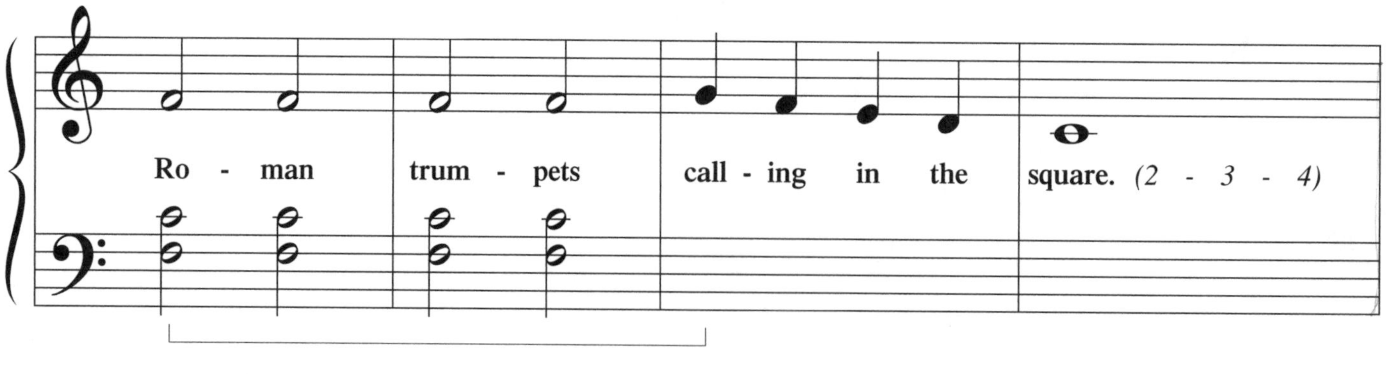

5

Ro - man trum - pets call - ing in the square. *(2 - 3 - 4)*

FF120

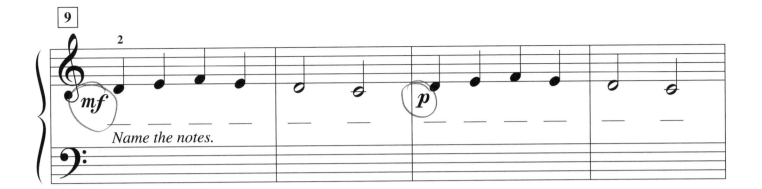

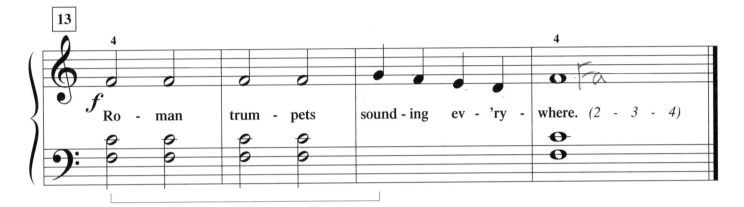

 CREATIVE Make up a short R.H. finger exercise using the C Pentascale (C-D-E-F-G) that moves up and down by **2nds**.

Teacher Duet: (Student plays *as written*. Teacher pedals for duet.)

Legato means smooth and connected, with no break in the sound.
To play *legato*, one finger goes down as the other finger comes up.

A **slur** is a curved line over or under a group of notes. It means to play *legato*.

- Play this example. *Listen* for a smooth, connected sound.

R.H.

slur

Repeat starting on HIGHER C's.

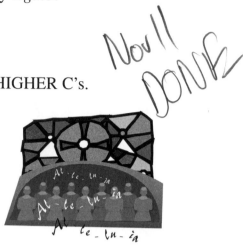

A monk singing this piece would take a breath at the
end of each slur. As you play this piece, let the music
"breathe" by lifting your wrist at the end of each slur.

Your teacher will show you how.

Chant of the Monk

Rather slowly, flowing

1 *on* ___?

f   Al - le - lu - ia,   Al - le - lu - ia,

4

Al - le - lu - ia. *(2 - 3 - 4)*   *p* Al - le - lu - ia,

8

Al - le - lu - ia,   Al - le - lu - ia. *(2 - 3 - 4)*

DISCOVERY

Name the notes of this piece aloud.

Teacher Duet: See bottom of page 25.

24

Theory p. 16

Playing Legato Hands Together

- Now play *Chant of the Monks* **hands together**.
  Your L.H. will play the same melody in a lower
  C Pentascale. Watch for changes of direction.

Notice the letter names stay the same, but the
finger numbers are different.

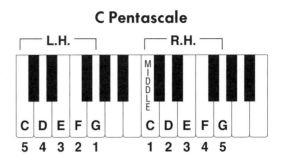

C Pentascale

Nov 11 DONE

Chant of the Monks

Rather slowly, flowing

DISCOVERY Which four measures move **down** by 2nds? *measures* ____, ____, ____, and ____
Which two measures move **up** by 2nds? *measures* ____ and ____
Which two measures move **up and down** by 2nds? *measures* ____ and ____

Teacher Duet: (Student plays *as written* for page 24; *1 octave higher* for page 25.)

FF1205

f-p on repeat

Learning Bass Clef G

Bass clef G is a space note.

It is a 2nd (step) above Bass Clef F.
(Remember, Bass Clef F is a Guide Note.)

NEW
space note

(Bass Clef F)

slur

Spinning steadily

Planetarium

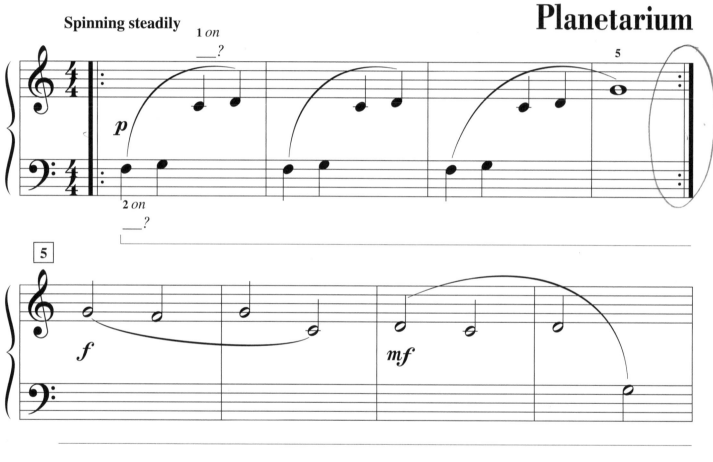

1 *on*
___?

2 *on*
___?

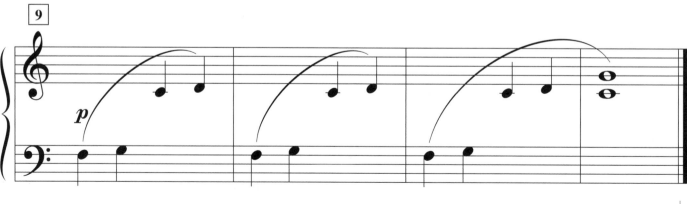

DISCOVERY

Name and play the 3 Guide Notes used in this piece.
Then name each note in the piece aloud.

Dotted Half Note

♩. = 3 counts (or beats)
Count "1 - 2 - 3"

A minuet is a stately dance in ¾ time, popular in the 1700s. George Washington danced the minuet.

Minuet

DISCOVERY

Point out four **accent marks** in this piece.

Teacher Duet: (Student plays *1 octave higher*)

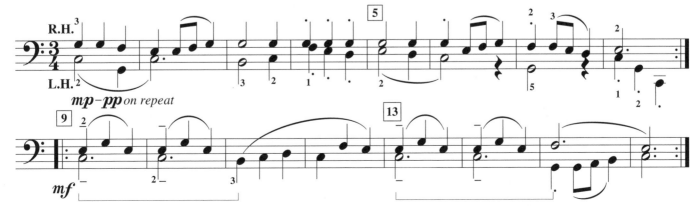

Sightreading pp. 15-17   Technique p. 16   Theory p. 19   Performance p. 3

Learning B and A

- Play B and A back and forth several times.
  Use L.H. fingers **1-2**, then **2-3**, then **3-4**.

- What is the interval
  between B and A? _____

line - space - line - space - line

__ __ B A __ __

- Name, then play the notes above.

Russian Folk Song

Traditional Russian
arranged

With spirit

3 *on* ___?
1 *on* ___?

2 *on* ___?

DISCOVERY Point out the echo in this piece.

Teacher Duet: (Student plays *1 octave higher*)

R.H.

L.H.

f-p on repeat

28

FF120

Sound Check: Are you observing the accent marks?

Midnight Ride

Fast, urgent

f

1 on ♩♩?

2 on ♩♩?

5

3

p

9

f

2

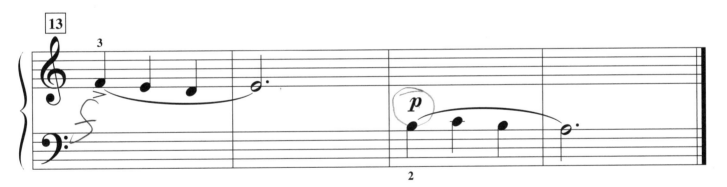

13

3

p

2

DISCOVERY Can you play this piece counting aloud, "1-2-3" for each measure?
Which beat is the strongest? **beat 1   beat 2   beat 3** *(circle one)*

Teacher Duet: (Student plays *1 octave higher*)

R.H.
mf

L.H.
mf

pp

5

9

13

pp

Performance p. 5   Theory p. 21   Technique p. 18

Reading 3rds (Skips) on the Staff

On the staff, a **3rd (skip)** moves from:

| **a LINE to the next LINE** | or | **a SPACE to the next SPACE** |

- Play this 3rd with R.H. fingers **1-3**, then **2-4**, then **3-5**.
- Play this 3rd with L.H. fingers **3-1**, then **4-2**, then **5-3**.

With a strong beat

Bus Stop Boogie

f Did-n't hear my | old a-larm clock. | Got-ta rush out | to the bus stop.

There's the bus now, | will I make it? | Hur-ry out the | door!

DISCOVERY Point out the measures with **line-to-line** 3rds.
Point out the measures with **space-to-space** 3rds.

Teacher Duet: (Student plays *1 octave higher*)

FF1205

Interval Check: Put a ✔ above each measure with the interval of a **3rd**.

Camptown Races

Stephen Foster
(1826–1864, U.S.)
arranged

Teacher Duet: (Student plays *1 octave higher*)

Quarter Rest 𝄽

The quarter rest = 1 beat of *silence*

- Clap or tap the rhythm below, counting aloud, "1 - 2 - 3 - 4."
  Hint: Count, but **do not clap** for the quarter rest.

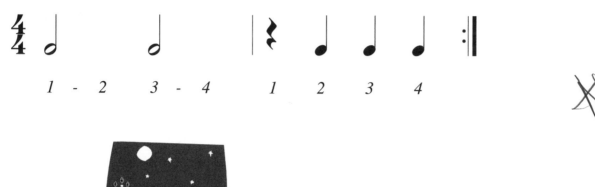

```
1 - 2   3 - 4   1   2   3   4
```

Eine Kleine Nachtmusik
(A Little Night Music)

Wolfgang Amadeus Mozart
(1756–1791, Austria)
arranged

With energy

1 *on* ___?

Count: 1 - 2 - 3 - 4   1 - 2 - 3 - 4   1 - 2 - 3 - 4   1 - 2 - 3 - 4

3 *on* Sol

Teacher Duet: (Student plays *1 octave higher*)

32

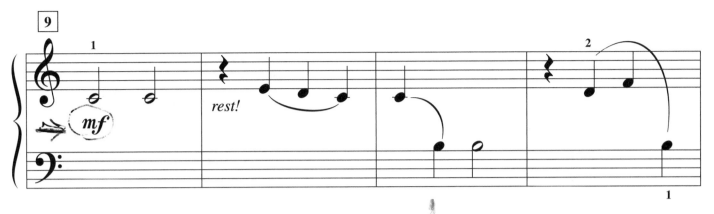

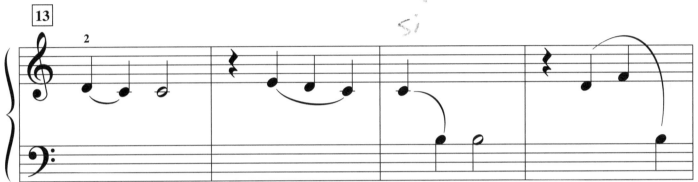

 Make up two measures of $\frac{4}{4}$ rhythm and write it below. Include a quarter rest.
Then clap or tap your rhythm.

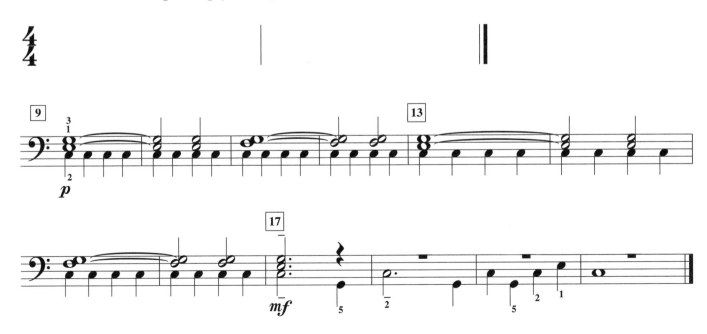

The Tie

A **tie** is a curved line connecting two notes on the
same line or space. It means the note will be played
once, but held for the length of both notes combined.

tie

$$= 8 \text{ beats}$$

DONE

Dec 2

Gypsy Band

Lively

3 *on* ___?
1 *on* ___?

Count: 1 - 2 - 3 - 4

mf

2 *on* ___?

5

4
2

Teacher Duet: (Student plays *1 octave higher*)

R.H.

4
2

5

4

3

1

3

1

3 2

L.H.

mp

1

4

5

1

3

3

1

4

3

3

1

3

2

5

34

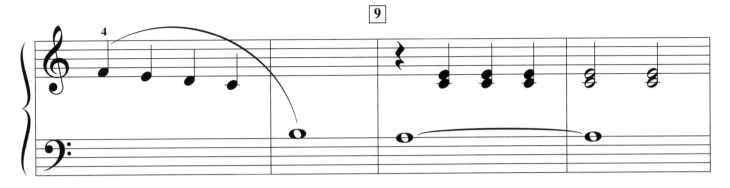

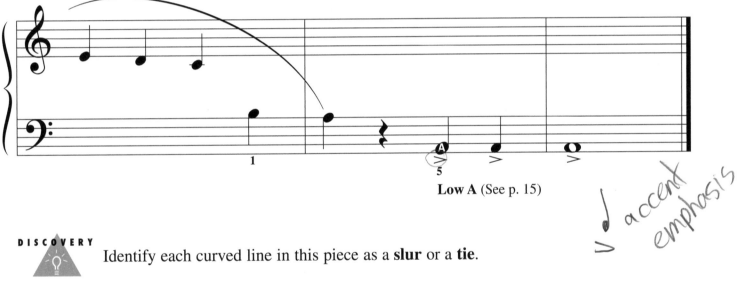

Low A (See p. 15)

 DISCOVERY Identify each curved line in this piece as a **slur** or a **tie**.

> ♩ accent
> emphasis

Eighth (8th) Notes

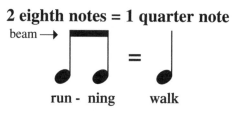

2 eighth notes = 1 quarter note

beam →

run - ning   walk

A single eighth note has a *flag*.

Think of eighth (8th) notes as *running* notes.
Two (or more) eighth notes are connected by a beam.

Directions: Clap or tap these rhythms with your teacher.
Two ways of counting are shown. Practice counting with each.

The Rhythm Flag

Feel a steady beat (pulse).

whole note
count: "1 - 2 - 3 - 4"

half notes
count: "1 - 2 "

quarter notes
count: "1"

eighth notes
count: "1 and"
Notice that each beat is
divided into two equal parts.

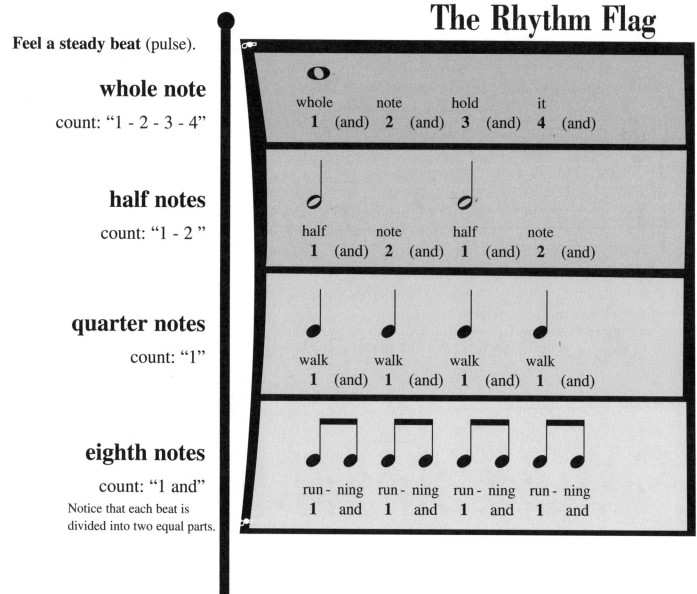

whole	note	hold	it
1 (and)	**2** (and)	**3** (and)	**4** (and)

half	note	half	note
1 (and)	**2** (and)	**1** (and)	**2** (and)

walk	walk	walk	walk
1 (and)	**1** (and)	**1** (and)	**1** (and)

run - ning	run - ning	run - ning	run - ning
1 and	**1** and	**1** and	**1** and

DISCOVERY

Clap the "Rhythm Flag" with the metronome ticking at: ♩ = 72   ♩ = 88   ♩ = 104.

Theory p. 26

FF1205

mp — mezzo piano
means moderately soft

Rhythm Check: Are your eighth notes flowing
gently, with a steady, even rhythm?

French Minuet

Jean-Philippe Rameau
(1683–1764, France)
arranged

DISCOVERY

Circle all the **3rds** in this piece. (Hint: There are eight.)

Teacher Duet: (Student plays *1 octave higher*)

Sightreading pp. 30–32   Technique p. 24   Performance p. 8

The Phrase

A *phrase* is a musical idea or thought.

A phrase is often shown in the music with a slur, also called a *phrase mark*.

Think of a phrase as a musical sentence and each note in the phrase as a word. Remember that all of the notes under the phrase mark are to be played as though each note is a meaningful word in the musical sentence.

phrase mark

- Point out each phrase in this piece.
- How many measures are in each phrase? ____

Morning

(from *Peer Gynt Suite*)

Edvard Grieg
(1843–1907, Norway)
arranged

Gently moving

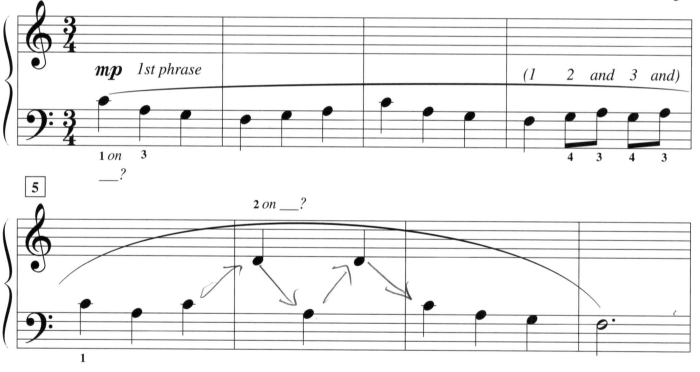

Teacher Duet: (Student plays *1 octave higher*)

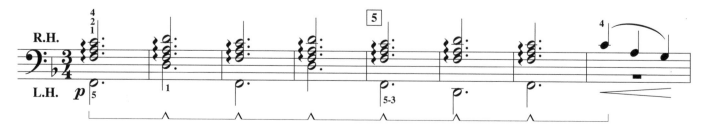

38

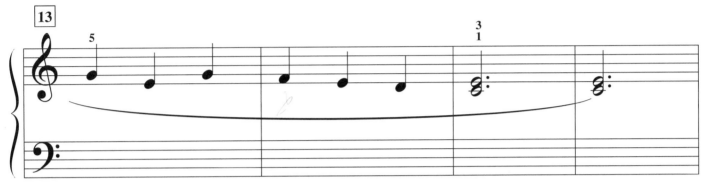

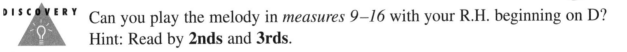

DISCOVERY Can you play the melody in *measures 9–16* with your R.H. beginning on D? Hint: Read by **2nds** and **3rds**.

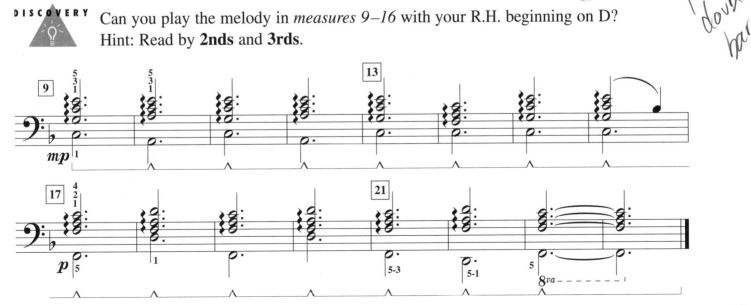

Pick-up Notes (or Upbeats)

This piece begins on *beat 4* with **pick-up notes**.
Pick-up note(s) lead into the first full measure.

If a piece begins with a pick-up, the last measure is
often incomplete. The combined beats of the incomplete
first and last measures will equal one full measure.

DONE
Dec 2

Oh! Susanna

Stephen C. Foster
(1826–1864, U.S.)
arranged

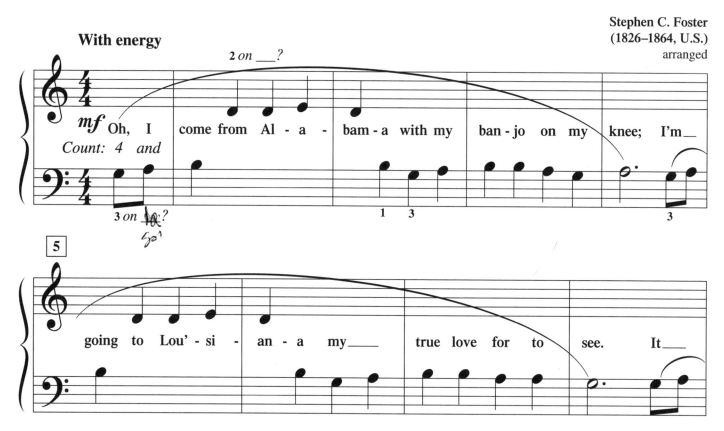

With energy

2 on ___?

mf Oh, I come from Al - a - bam - a with my ban - jo on my knee; I'm__

Count: 4 and

3 on ___?

5 going to Lou' - si - an - a my__ true love for to see. It__

Teacher Duet: (Student plays *1 octave higher*)

R.H.

L.H. *mf*

40

FF1205

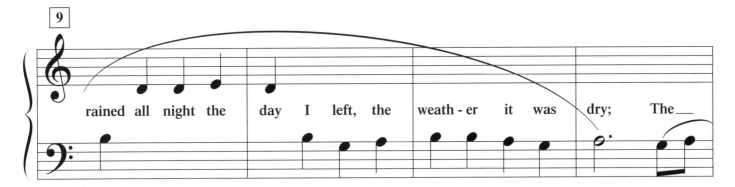

rained all night the day I left, the weath-er it was dry; The__

sun so hot I froze to death, Su - san - na don't you cry.

Oh! Su - san - na, Oh, don't you cry for me, For I've

f

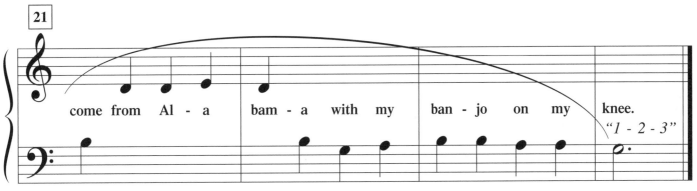

come from Al - a bam - a with my ban - jo on my knee.

"1 - 2 - 3"

DISCOVERY How many phrases are in this piece? _____

Point out the phrase that begins differently than the others.

New Guide Note: Bass C

- Number the **bass clef spaces 1-2-3-4** in the bass staff shown.
  (Spaces are numbered from bottom to top. See p. 14.)
  Which space is Bass C? _____ This is your new Guide Note.

- Practice leaping from *Middle C* to *Bass C* with
  L.H. fingers 1 and 5.
  This distance is the interval of an **octave** (8 notes).

Middle C

Bass C
(New Guide Note)

Guide Note Review

- On the staff above, draw whole notes
  on **Treble Clef G** and **Bass Clef F**.

- Then play these four Guide Notes on the piano.

Jump Shots

(for L.H. alone)

Bouncy

mf

1 *on*
___?   5   1   5   1

5

mf

1   5

DISCOVERY   Find and play other **octaves** on the keyboard with your L.H. (Use fingers 5 and 1.)

FF1205

Bass C Pentascale

Learn these notes that step up from Guide Note **Bass C**.
(You already know the circled notes.)

Locomotive Rhythms

(for L.H. only)

DONE

- First clap or tap, counting aloud.

DISCOVERY Play *Locomotive Rhythms* **hands together**. The R.H. plays in a *higher* C Pentascale.

Teacher Duet: (Student plays *1 octave higher*)

FF1205

Theory p. 31   Technique pp. 28, 30

A **theme** (melody) often has several musical phrases.

- How many phrases are in this famous theme *(measures 1–16)* by Beethoven? _____

Ode to Joy

(Theme from the 9th Symphony*)

C Pentascale

Ludwig van Beethoven
(1770–1827, Germany)
arranged

*A *symphony* is a large-scale work for orchestra. It is a mark of Beethoven's genius that he wrote this masterpiece after he had gone deaf.

A *thin* double bar shows the end of a section.

FF1205

Sightreading pp. 39-41

Theory pp. 32-33

Performance pp. 10-11

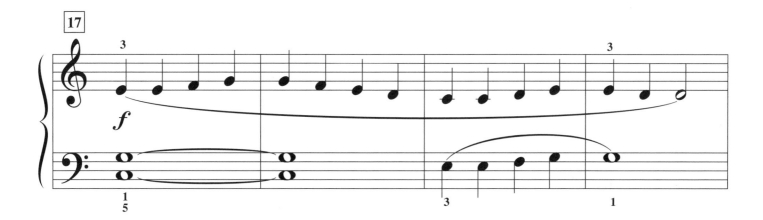

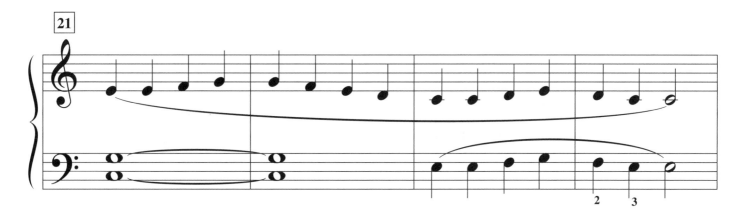

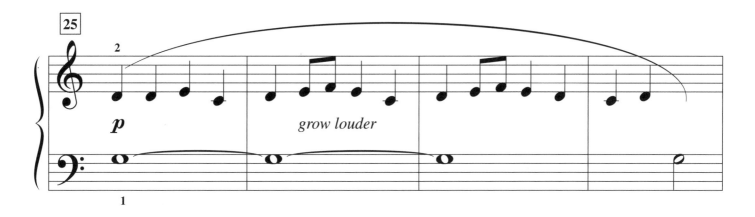

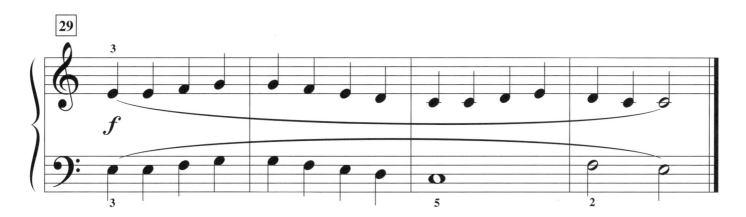

DISCOVERY

Where is the opening left-hand phrase played by the right hand? *measure* _____

Staccato means a crisp, detached sound.

To play *staccato*, quickly bring the finger off the key.

The staccato mark is a small dot placed above or below the note.

2 beats per measure

R.H.
Warm-up

Bounc- ing gent- ly, bounc- ing gent- ly, bounc- ing down the keys.

mf-p on repeat

L.H.
Warm-up

Bounc- ing gent- ly, bounc- ing gent- ly, bounc- ing down the keys.

mf-p on repeat

Staccato Check: Is your wrist loose and relaxed as you play staccato?

Theme from the

"Surprise" Symphony

Franz Joseph Haydn
(1732–1809, Austria)
arranged

Lightly

1 *on* ___?

p

5 *on* ___?

A circled finger number alerts you to a change of hand position.

f

CREATIVE Make up a short "raindrop" melody with the C Pentascale.
Play high on the keyboard with all notes *staccato*.

Theory p.34 Technique pp. 28, 31

This piece uses both **legato** and **staccato** touches.
Hint: Play the thumb on the *side tip*.

Hungarian Dance

Johannes Brahms
(1833–1897, Germany)
arranged

Teacher Duet: (Student plays *1 octave higher*)

Performance p. 12   Technique pp. 29, 32   Sightreading pp. 42-44

Learning Treble Clef A

(Treble G)

Treble Clef A is a space note.
It is a 2nd *above* Treble Clef G.
(Remember, Treble Clef G is
a Guide Note.)

Irish Washerwoman

Hint: Watch for the change in hand
position at *measures 6* and 9.

Traditional
arranged

Teacher Duet: (Student plays *as written*)

48

To help you with the R.H. position changes,
play the **first R.H. note** in each measure.
(Notice the R.H. begins in the bass clef.)

Your teacher will demonstrate.

Waltz

Frédéric Chopin
(1810–1849, Poland)
arranged

Sightreading pp. 45-47

Technique pp. 29, 34

Theory p. 35

Teacher Duet: (Student plays *2 octaves* higher)

FACE the Spaces

The space notes on the treble staff spell the word **F A C E**.
(You have already learned the treble F and A space notes.)

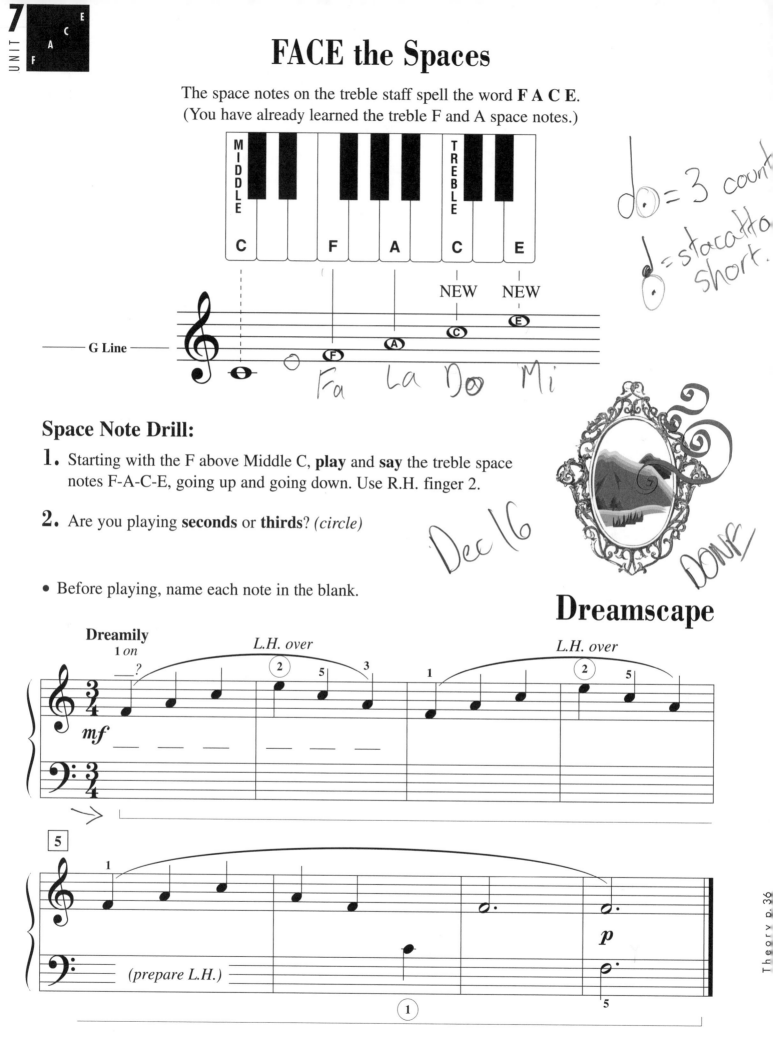

— G Line —

handwritten: do. = 3 count
handwritten: ♩ = stacatto short.

NEW   NEW

handwritten: Fa La Do Mi

Space Note Drill:

1. Starting with the F above Middle C, **play** and **say** the treble space notes F-A-C-E, going up and going down. Use R.H. finger 2.

2. Are you playing **seconds** or **thirds**? *(circle)*

handwritten: Dec 16

handwritten: DONE

- Before playing, name each note in the blank.

Dreamscape

Dreamily
1 *on*

mf

L.H. over

L.H. over

5

(prepare L.H.)

p

Theory p. 36

CREATIVE
With damper pedal down, create your own "Dreamscape" using treble F - A - C - E.

FF1205

Halftime Show

Moderately fast

Up the field they come, march-ing band at half-time.
Down the field they go, march-ing band at half time.

Hav-ing so much fun play-ing at the game.
What a mu-sic show for the foot-ball game!

The Lonely Pine

Very slow and lonely

mf

p (echo softly)

move ① *to F*

stay

(prepare R.H.)

mf

p

Sightreading pp. 48-50

Technique p. 36

Half Rest (sits *above* line 3)

The half rest = **2 beats of silence**

Count: "1   2   3   4"

Whole Rest (hangs *below* line 4.)

The whole rest = rest for any **whole measure**.

4 beats of silence   **3 beats** of silence

Rest Check: Identify each rest for *measures 9–12.*

Racecar Rally

Zipping along

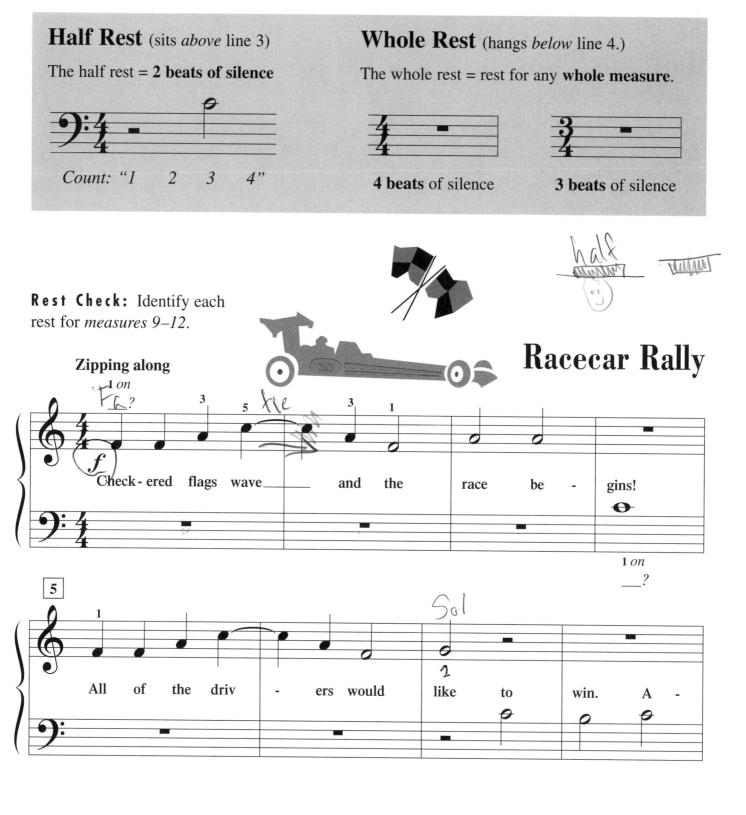

Check - ered flags wave_____ and the race be - gins!

All of the driv - ers would like to win. A -

Teacher Duet: (Student plays *1 octave higher*)

R.H.

L.H.   *mf*

52

round and a - round _____ they speed, each tries to take _____ the lead.

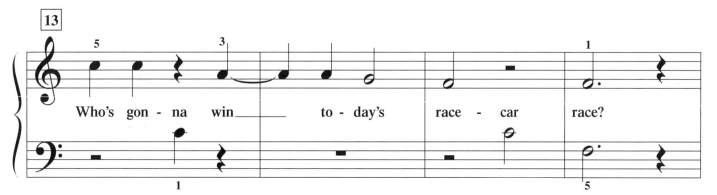

Who's gon - na win _____ to - day's race - car race?

"Four" just came 'round _____ the bend, "Ten" takes the lead _____ a - gain,

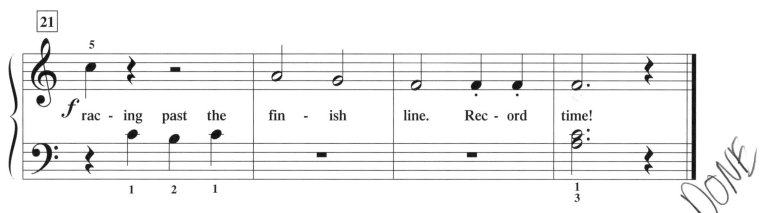

f rac - ing past the fin - ish line. Rec - ord time!

DISCOVERY What is "racecar" spelled backwards? _____ Put the racecar in reverse by playing the piece backwards, from *measure 24* to *measure 21*. This is called **retrograde**.

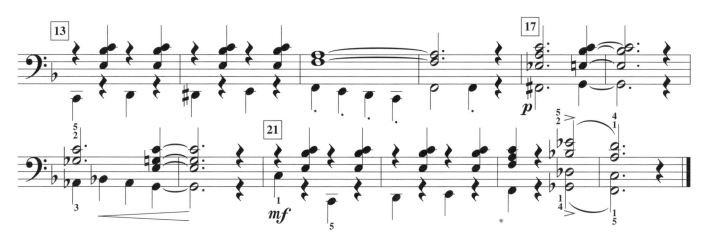

New Guide Note: Treble C

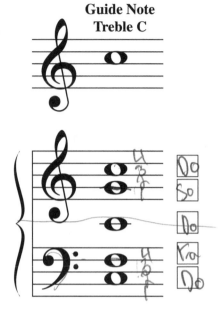

Guide Note Treble C

- Number the **treble clef spaces 1-2-3-4** in the treble staff shown. Which space is Treble C? _____ This is your new Guide Note.

- Practice leaping from *Middle C* to *Treble C* with R.H. fingers 1 and 5. What is the name of this interval? _____

Guide Note Review

"Guide notes" are your "anchors" as you learn new notes on the staff.

You can name any note on the staff by *stepping up* or *down* from Guide Notes.

- Name, then play these Guide Notes.

Guide Note Pinball

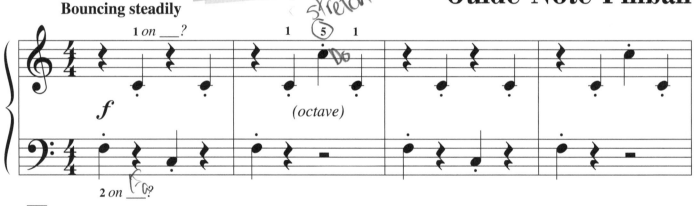

Bouncing steadily

(octave)

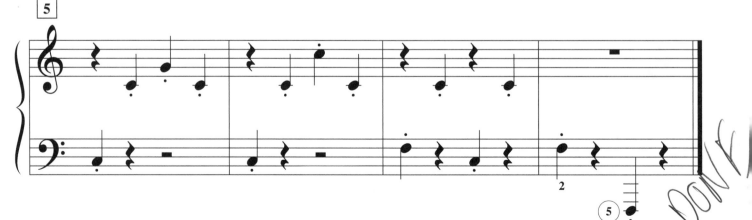

Play the lowest F on the keyboard.

DISCOVERY   Play *up a 3rd* from **Treble C**.   Play *down a 2nd* from **Treble G**.
Play *up a 2nd* from **Bass F**.   Play *down a 3rd* from **Bass C**.

Treble C Pentascale

Learn these notes that *step up* from Guide Note **Treble C**.
(You already know the circled notes.)

- Play and say: **Treble C**   **D**   **E**   **F**   **G**

                space - line - space - line - space

Learn and play this piece by:

- reading **2nds**, **3rds**, and **repeated notes**
- recognizing note names Treble C-D-E-F-G

English Minuet

Alexander Reinagle
(1756–1809, England)
transposed to C major

Stately

Teacher Duet: (Student plays *1 octave higher*)

Sightreading pp. 54-56

Technique p. 38

Theory p. 41

F1205

55

2

Sol La Sol
Mi Fa Fa Do
Do Do Si
I IV V Dec 16

8va — Octave Sign (ottava)

When 8va is written below the staff, play one octave (8 notes) *lower* than written. When 8va is written above the staff, play one octave *higher*.

Bagpipes

C Pentascale

Lively

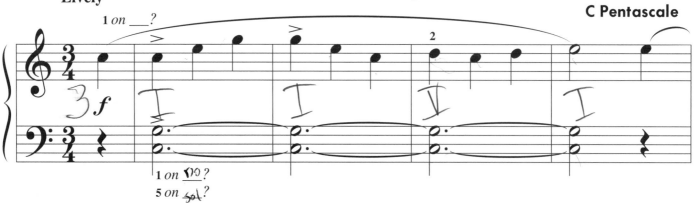

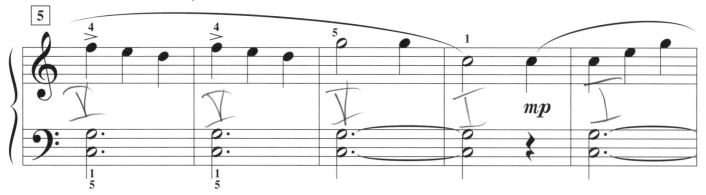

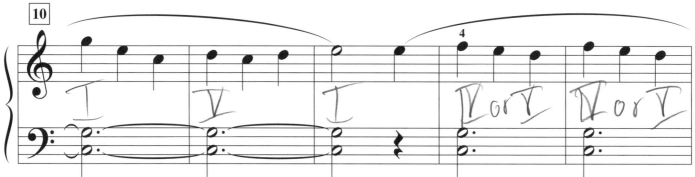

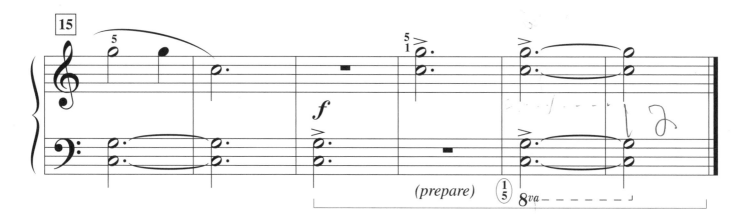

DISCOVERY

Which two phrases begin with **3rds**? Which two phrases begin with **2nds**?

FF120

Imitation

Notice that each phrase for the L.H. is "copied"
by the R.H. This is called *imitation*.

Dec 16

Two-Hand Conversation

Moderately

1 *on*
___?   **Name the pentascale.** _____

5 *on*
___?

3

(prepare R.H.)

5

(prepare R.H.)

7

(prepare R.H.)

DONE

Sightreading pp. 57-59

Technique p. 39

CREATIVE
Make up a one-measure melody with your L.H. in the C Pentascale.
Imitate the melody with your R.H. one octave *higher*. Try several of these.

Finding Imitation

- Which hand imitates in *measures 1–4*?
  R.H. or L.H. *(circle)*
- Which hand imitates in *measures 17–20*?
  R.H. or L.H. *(circle)*

Jan 13

When the Saints Go Marching In

Name the pentascale. _____

Traditional

FF1205

DISCOVERY Write the counts in the music for the first and last *incomplete measures*.

DONE 01/27/16

More About Intervals

Intervals are easy to measure at the keyboard.

Count the **number of white keys** (letter names) including the *first* and *last*. This is the number (size) of the interval.

You have already learned the intervals of a **2nd** and a **3rd**.

Review:

2nd

C D

1   2   = 2nd

3rd

C E

1   2   3   = 3rd

New:

A **4th** spans 4 letter names.

C   F

1   2   3   4   = 4th

A **5th** spans 5 letter names.

C   G

1   2   3   4   5   = 5th

4ths move up or down from:

a **line to a space** or a **space to a line**

Think: skip + a step

• Play:

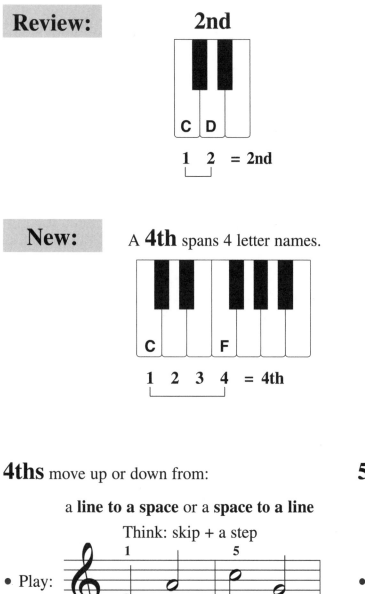

4th up   4th down

• What other interval have you learned that moves from a **line to space** or a **space to line**? _____

5ths move up or down from:

a **line to a line** or a **space to a space**

Think: skip + a skip

• Play:

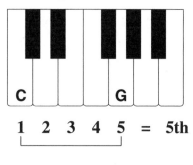

5th up   5th down

• What other interval have you learned that moves from a **line to line** or a **space to space**? _____

DISCOVERY

A **4th** sounds like the opening of "Here Comes the Bride."
A **5th** sounds like the opening of "Twinkle, Twinkle, Little Star."
Your teacher will play some **4ths** and **5ths**. *Listen* and practice identifying each.

(**Teacher Note:** Play the notes separately, then together.)

FF120

Focus on Fourths (4ths)

To draw an interval, count the starting note and each line and space.

- Draw a **4th** above these line notes.
- Draw a **4th** above these space notes.

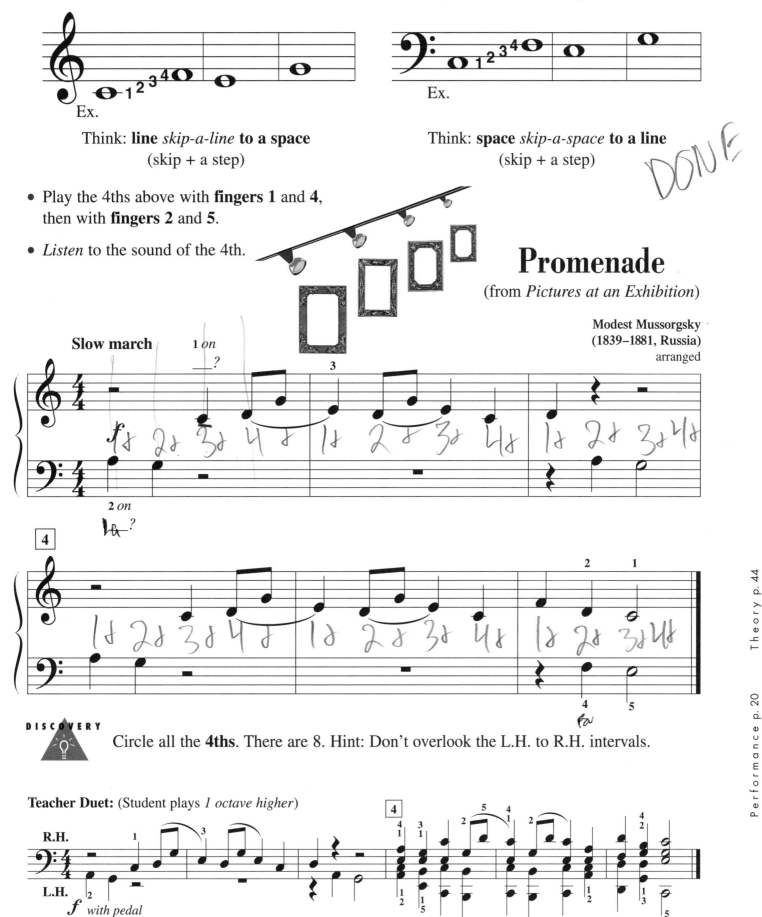

Ex.   Ex.

Think: **line** *skip-a-line* **to a space**   Think: **space** *skip-a-space* **to a line**
(skip + a step)   (skip + a step)

DONE

- Play the 4ths above with **fingers 1** and **4**, then with **fingers 2** and **5**.

- *Listen* to the sound of the 4th.

Promenade
(from *Pictures at an Exhibition*)

Modest Mussorgsky
(1839–1881, Russia)
arranged

Slow march

DISCOVERY

Circle all the **4ths**. There are 8. Hint: Don't overlook the L.H. to R.H. intervals.

Teacher Duet: (Student plays *1 octave higher*)

R.H.

L.H. *f* with pedal

Performance p. 20   Theory p. 44   **61**

- Which R.H. finger is not played in this piece? _____

Chinese Dragon

C Pentascale

(move down quickly)

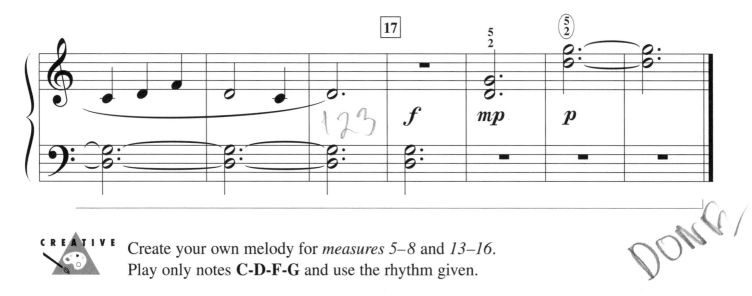

CREATIVE Create your own melody for *measures 5–8* and *13–16*.
Play only notes **C-D-F-G** and use the rhythm given.

62

Focus on Fifths (5ths)

- Draw a **5th** above these line notes.

Ex.

- Draw a **5th** above these space notes.

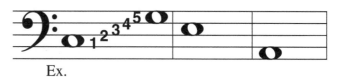

Ex.

Think: **line** *skip-a-line* **to a line**
(skip + a skip)

Think: **space** *skip-a-space* **to a space**
(skip + a skip)

Feb 3

- Play the 5ths above.
  Listen to the open sound of the 5th.

The King of Hearts

DISCOVERY

Name two intervals that move
line-to-line or **space-to-space**.
_____ and _____

1st and 2nd Endings

Play the 1st ending and take the repeat. Then play the 2nd ending, skipping over the 1st ending.

Teacher Duet: (Student plays *1 octave higher*)

DONE 02/10/6

FF120

No Moon Tonight

Smoothly moving

Lyrics:
No moon to - night, no moon to - night.
Still - ness fills the dark eve - ning sky,
no moon to - night.

Teacher Duet: (Student plays *1 octave higher*)

Theory p. 47   Technique p. 45

Musical Form

The overall structure of a piece is called musical form.

This piece has three sections: **section A**, **section B**, and the return of **section A**. It is in **A B A form**.

- Find and label these three sections in the music.
  Hint: The B section is *different* from the A section and gives variety to the piece.

Forest Drums includes an optional drum part.

Play this rhythm part using a bongo or conga drum, a percussion setting on a digital keyboard, or tapping on your lap as your teacher plays the piano part.*

Count carefully!

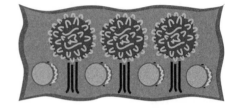

Forest Drums

Notice the different hand position.

*A rubber bucket or large metal canister may also be used as a drum.

DISCOVERY

Name each type of **rest** in the drum part for *measure 1–8*.

The Sharp ♯

A **half step** is from one
key to the very *closest* key.

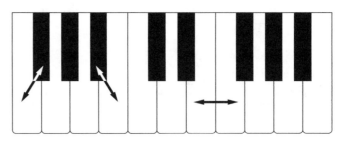

- Play these **half steps** on the piano.
- Find and play several more half steps.

A **sharp** means to play the key
that is a **half step HIGHER**.

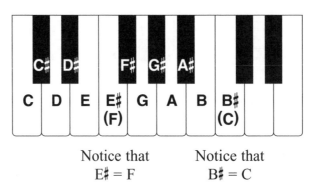

Notice that   Notice that
E♯ = F   B♯ = C

- Play these keys on the keyboard while naming them aloud.
- Your teacher will call out the names of **sharp keys**.
  Find and play each on the keyboard.

Guide Note Review

- Name, then play
  these Guide Notes.

- Name, then play these **sharped** Guide Notes.
  Notice the sharp is written *in front of* the note
  and is on the same line or space.

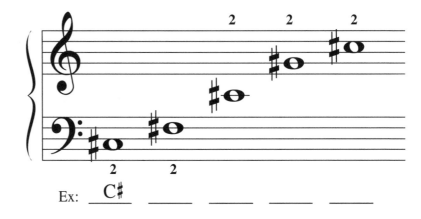

Ex: ___C♯___ _____ _____ _____ _____

DISCOVERY With L.H. finger 2, play from *Bass C* to *Middle C* moving UP by **half steps**.
Say the key names aloud.
(C - C♯ - D - D♯ - E - F - F♯ - G - G♯ - A - A♯ - B - C)

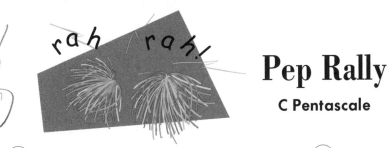

Pep Rally
C Pentascale

First play hands alone.

Feb 3/10

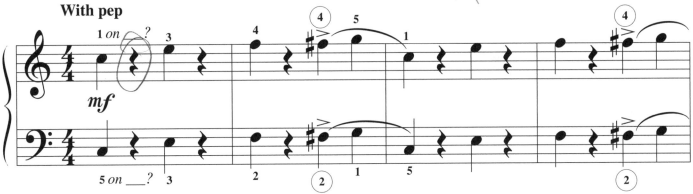

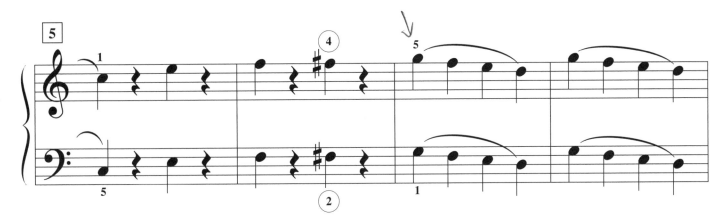

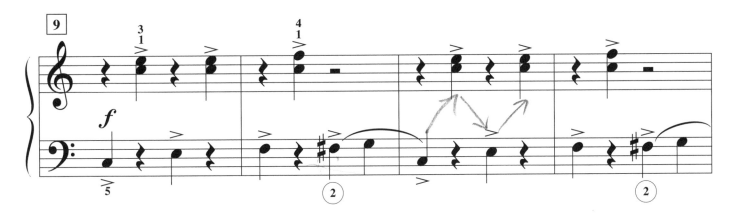

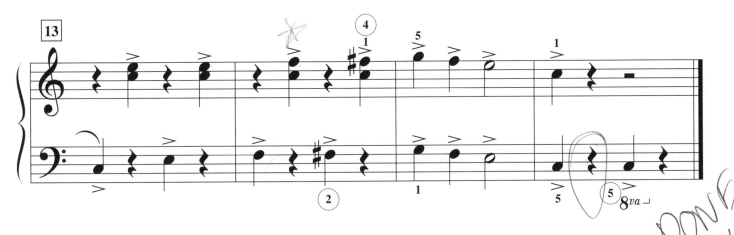

Sightreading pp. 69-71

Theory p. 50

DONE
02/23/14

 CREATIVE Explore the range of the keyboard. Play the R.H. of *Pep Rally* in a HIGHER
C Pentascale than written, while the L.H. plays in a LOWER C Pentascale.

The word **dynamics** comes from the Greek word for "power."
In music, *dynamics* mean the "louds and softs" of the sound.

p, *mp*, *mf*, and *f* are dynamic marks you have learned.

Feb 10

New Dynamic Marks

crescendo *(cresc.)* ————————— play gradually louder
(pronounced kreh-SHEN-doh)

diminuendo *(dim.)* ————————— play gradually softer
(pronounced di-min-u-EN-doh)

This symbol is also called *decrescendo* (day-kreh-SHEN-doh).

A sharp carries through an entire measure,
but not past a bar line. (See *measure 3*.)

In a new measure, the sharp must be written again.

Go Down Moses

Slowly, soulfully

Spiritual
arranged

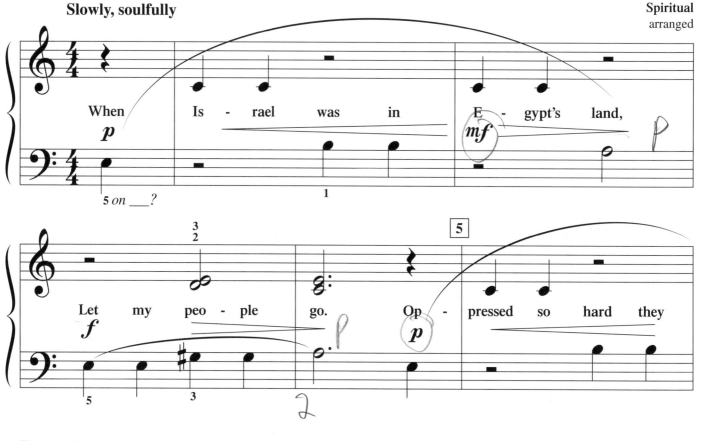

Teacher Duet: (Student plays *1 octave higher*)

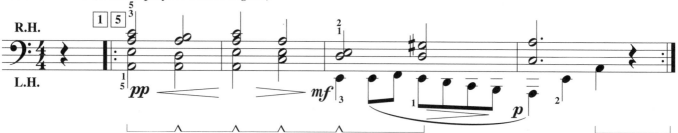

FF120

DISCOVERY Find a measure where only *one* sharped note is played.
Find three measures where *two* sharped notes are played.

DONE
02/23/6

The Flat ♭

A **flat** means to play the key that is a **half step LOWER**.

Notice that
F♭ = E

Notice that
C♭ = B

- Play these keys on the keyboard while naming them aloud.
- Your teacher will call out the names of **flat keys**. Find and play each on the keyboard.

A flat carries through an entire measure, but not past a bar line.

In a new measure, the flat must be written again.

still E♭

Feb 10

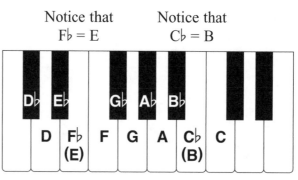

Zum Gali Gali

Israeli Folk Song
arranged

With energy

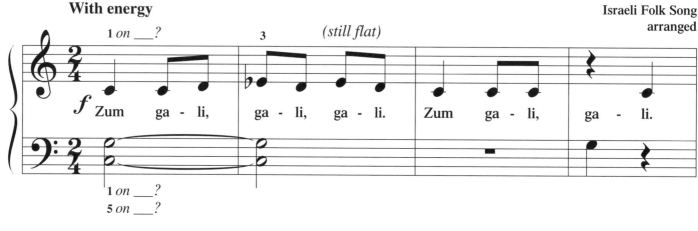

1 on ___?

3

(still flat)

f Zum ga - li, ga - li, ga - li. Zum ga - li, ga - li.

1 on ___?
5 on ___?

Teacher Duet: (Student plays *1 octave higher*)

R.H.

L.H.

mf

p

cresc.

mf

f

72

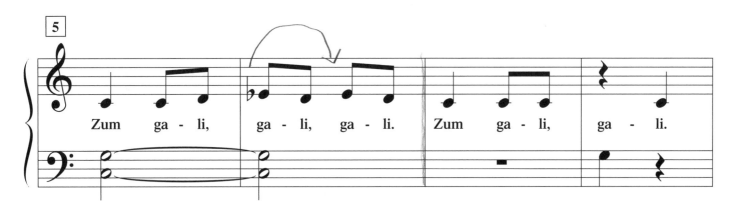

5

Zum ga - li, ga - li, ga - li. Zum ga - li, ga - li.

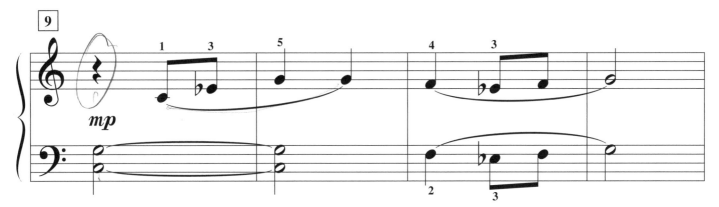

9

mp

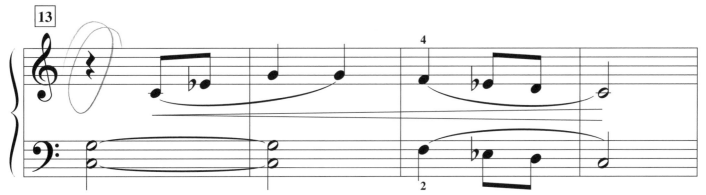

13

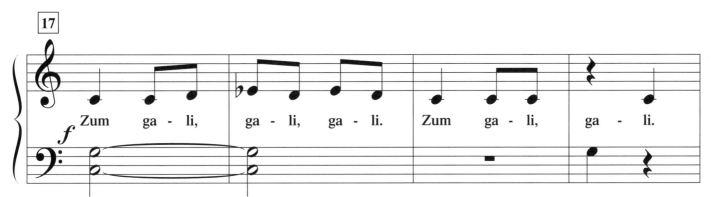

17

f Zum ga - li, ga - li, ga - li. Zum ga - li, ga - li.

21

Zum ga - li, ga - li, ga - li. Zum! Zum! Zum!

DONE
02/23/16

D I S C O V E R Y

Choose any 4 black keys. Tell your teacher the **flat name** and **sharp name** of each.

The Natural

A natural cancels a sharp or a flat.
A natural is always a white key.

● Play:

Feb24

 # sharp
♭ flat
♮ natural

Sometimes a natural is written as a reminder to play
a white key in a new measure. (See *measure 4.*)

Sugarfoot Rag

Scott Joplin

Happily

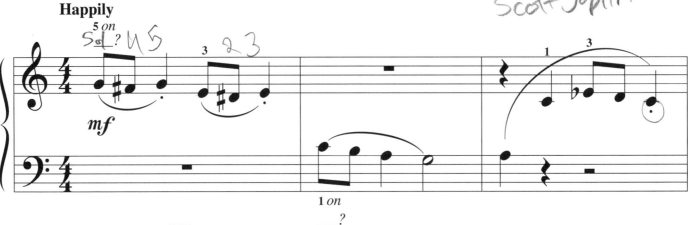

Teacher Duet: (Student plays *1 octave higher*)

74

FF120

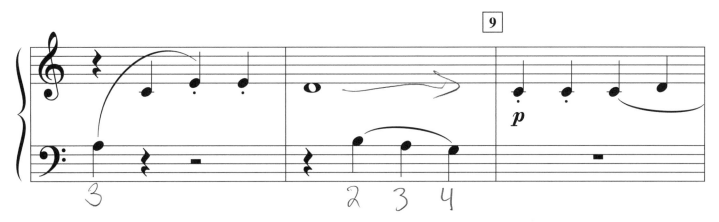

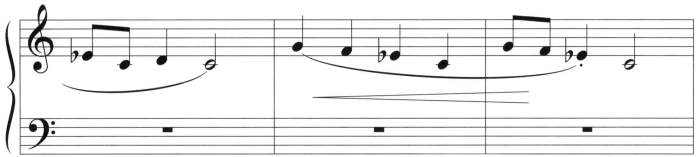

DISCOVERY

What interval is played by the R.H. in the last measure? _____

DONE 03/16/16

C Pentascale Warm-up

Hands Together

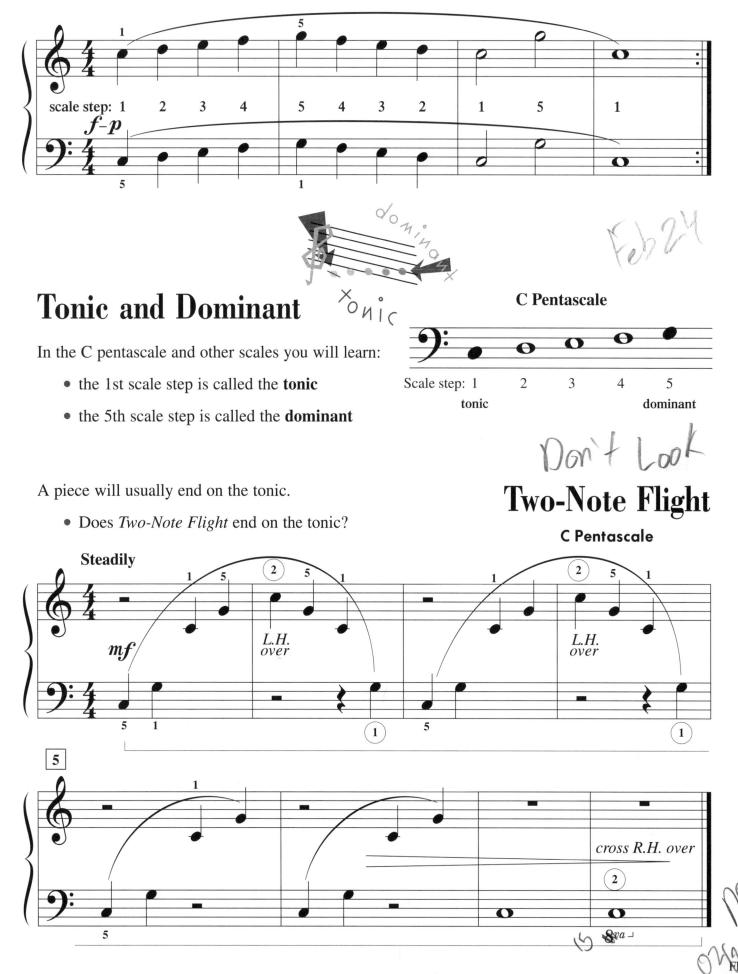

scale step: 1 2 3 4 5 4 3 2 1 5 1

f–p

Tonic and Dominant

In the C pentascale and other scales you will learn:

- the 1st scale step is called the **tonic**
- the 5th scale step is called the **dominant**

A piece will usually end on the tonic.

- Does *Two-Note Flight* end on the tonic?

C Pentascale

Scale step: 1 2 3 4 5

tonic   dominant

Feb 24

Don't Look

Two-Note Flight

C Pentascale

Steadily

mf

L.H. over

L.H. over

5

cross R.H. over

FF1207

rit. = *ritardando*

This means a gradual slowing of the music.
Ritardando is often shortened to *ritard.* or *rit.*

Journey by Camel

C Pentascale

DISCOVERY

Put a check ✔ above the measures that use only **tonic** and **dominant** notes.

Teacher Duet: (Student plays *as written*)

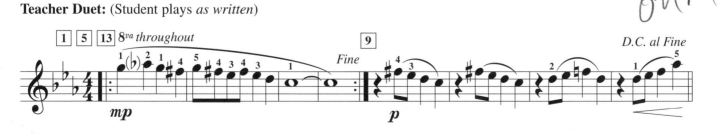

Sightreading pp. 78-80

Technique p. 52

Theory p. 54

Performance p. 28

The C Chord

Three or more tones played together form a *chord*.

The C chord is made of 3 tones
that build up in **3rds** from C.

- C is the **root**
- E is the **3rd**
- G is the **5th**

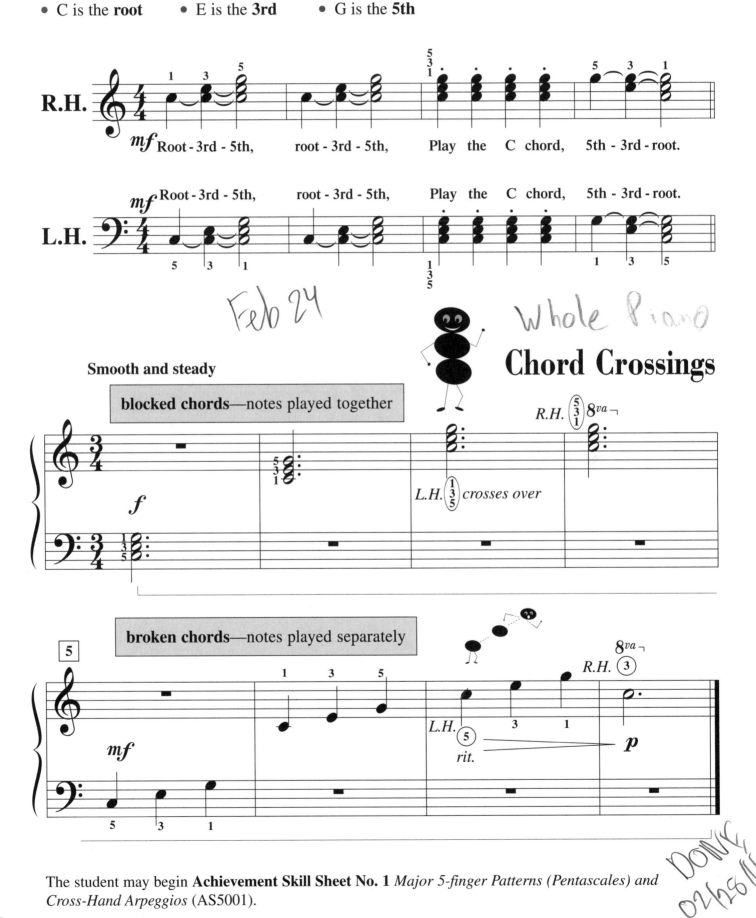

The student may begin **Achievement Skill Sheet No. 1** *Major 5-finger Patterns (Pentascales) and Cross-Hand Arpeggios (AS5001).*

FF12

REVIEW: C is the **tonic note** in the key of C.

NEW: The C chord is the **tonic chord** in the key of C because it is built on the tonic note.

It is commonly called the **I chord**.
(**I** is the Roman numeral for the number "1".)

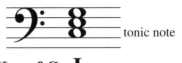

Feb 24

Key of C: I — tonic note

- Before playing this piece, write the Roman numeral **I** under each measure with a *blocked* or *broken* C chord.

*pedal
*dynamics

Row, Row, Row Your Boat

C Pentascale

Traditional
arranged

Lively

Row, row, row your boat gent - ly
mp

down the stream. Mer - ri - ly, mer - ri - ly,
crescendo
mf
L.H. over
R.H.

mer - ri - ly, mer - ri - ly, Life is but a dream.
p

Sightreading pp. 81-83

Technique p. 53

DONE
03/23/16

CREATIVE Play *Row, Row, Row Your Boat* as a round with your teacher. The teacher plays 2 octaves *higher* than written and begins after the student plays 4 measures. Student and teacher play two times.

Form Check:

The form of this piece is **A A B A**.

- Label the sections in your music.
  Hint: Notice the repeat of section A.

I've Got Music

Name the pentascale. _____

Moderate beat

1 on ___?

f

| I | tell | my | hon | - | ey |
| I | love | to | sing | | it, |

| I | don't | have | mon | - | ey, |
| to | sway | and | swing | | it. |

1 on ___?
3 on ___?
5 on ___?

5 | 13

but I've got mu - sic down in my soul.
Yes, I've got mu - sic down in my soul.

Teacher Duet: (Student plays *1 octave higher*)

FF120

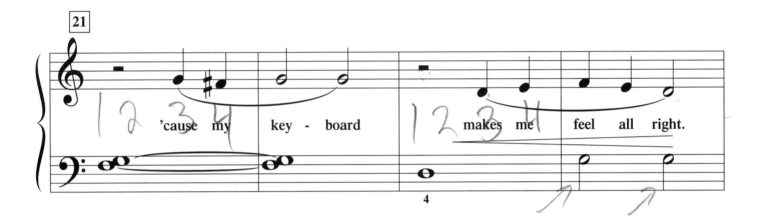

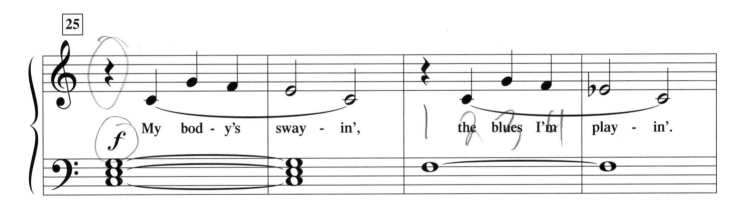

ritardando = slow down

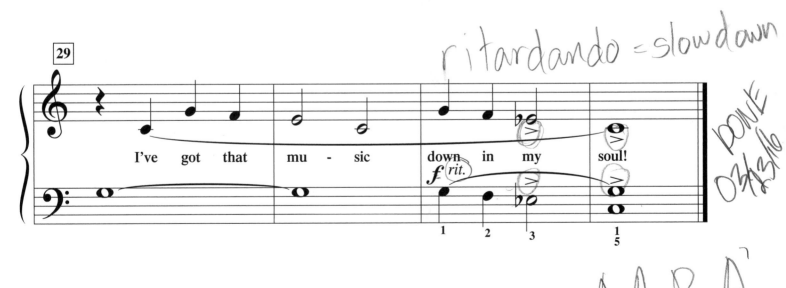

AABA

DISCOVERY At the end of the **B section** *(measure 24)*, does the L.H. play the **tonic note** or **dominant note**? _____

The V⁷ Chord in the Key of C

(pronounced "five-seven")

V is the Roman numeral for the number 5.

The **V⁷** chord is a 4-note chord built up in 3rds from the **dominant**.

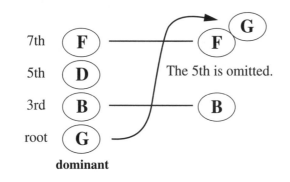

7th	F → F	G
5th	D	The 5th is omitted.
3rd	B → B	
root	G	

dominant

> The notes of the V⁷ chord are often rearranged to form a **3-note chord**.

V⁷ for Left Hand

- First play a 5th in the C Pentascale.

- Move finger 5 a **half step lower** (B).
  (This expands the interval to a 6th.)

- Add **finger 2** (step 4) from the C pentascale.

V⁷ for Right Hand

- First play a 5th in the C Pentascale.

- Move finger 1 a **half step lower** (B).
  (This expands the interval to a 6th.)

- Add **finger 4** (step 4) from the C pentascale.

Melody and Harmony

The *melody* is the tune. *Harmony* refers to the notes or chords played with the melody.

- Practice this **I** and **V⁷** harmony warm-up.

Harmony Sounds
(blocked chords)

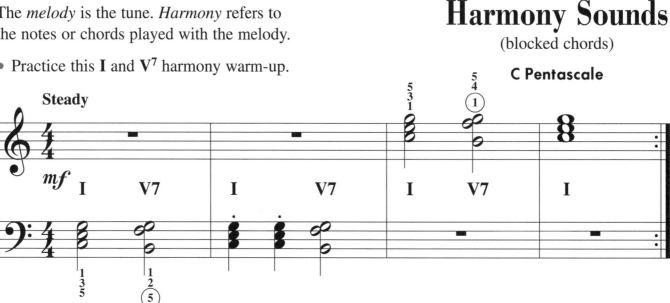

DISCOVERY Play a **C pentascale** up and down s-l-o-w-l-y with your R.H.
Harmonize *each* note by playing a **I** or **V⁷** chord with your L.H.
Listen and let your ears guide you.

82

Prince of Denmark's March
(A Trumpet Voluntary)

C Pentascale

Jeremiah Clarke
(1673–1707, England)
arranged

DISCOVERY

Analyze the harmony by writing **I** or **V⁷** below each chord.

Teacher Duet: (Student plays *1 octave higher*)

Warm-up: Practice the
L.H. alone for *measures 3–5.*

March 23

Amazing Grace

Words by John Newton
Early American melody
arranged

Gently moving

1 on ___?

A - maz - ing_____ grace, how

1 on ___?

3   **5**

sweet   the   sound   that   saved   a_____

2 *(extend thumb)* ①   2   2

wretch   like   me!_____   I   **f**

①⑤

Teacher Duet: (Student plays *1 octave higher*)

R.H.

L.H.   *p*

(teacher pedals)

5

84

FF120

once   was_____   lost,   but

(lift)   ④

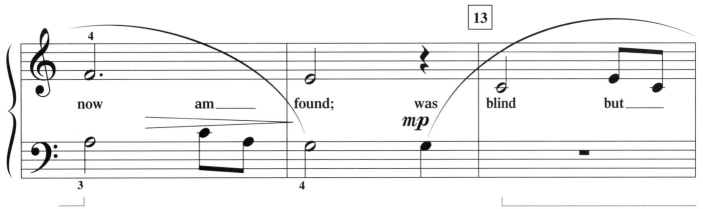

now   am_____   found;   was   blind   but_____

mp

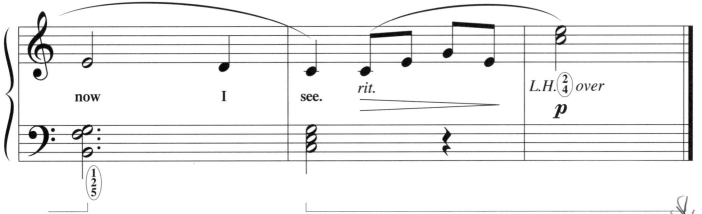

now   I   see. *rit.*

L.H. $\frac{2}{4}$ *over*

p

D I S C O V E R Y

Where does the R.H. play a **broken chord**? *measure* _____

DONE
03/30/16

p

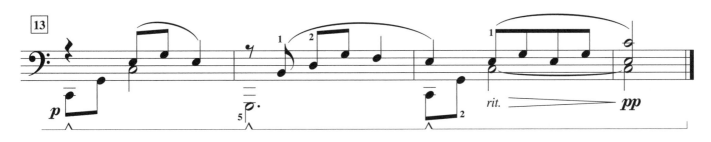

p   *rit.*   *pp*

Reading in Three G Pentascales

The 5 notes of the **G Pentascale** are **G A B C D**.

- Find these 3 G Pentascales on the piano.

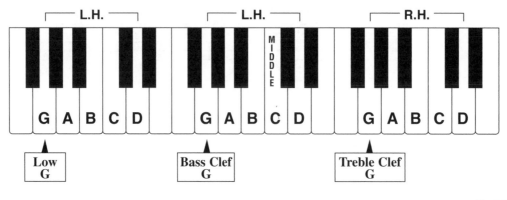

G Pentascales

- Play each **G Pentascale** and exercise below.

DONE 03/23/16

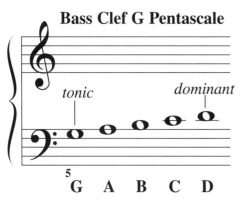

Low G Pentascale

tonic   dominant

5
G   A   B   C   D

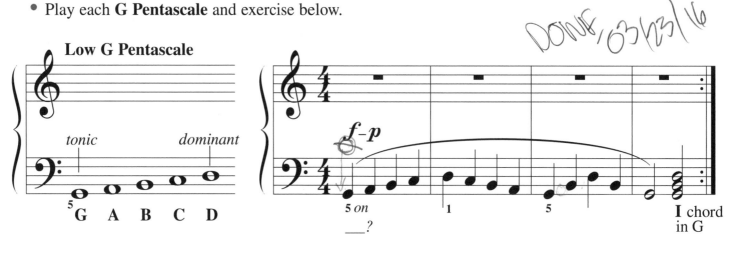

f–p

5 on ___ ?   1   5   **I** chord in G

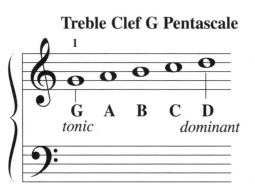

Bass Clef G Pentascale

tonic   dominant

5
G   A   B   C   D

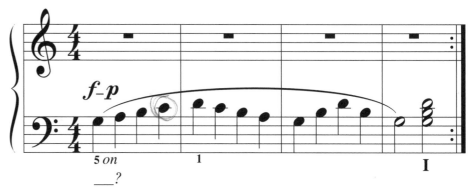

f–p

5 on ___ ?   1   **I**

Treble Clef G Pentascale

1
G   A   B   C   D
tonic   dominant

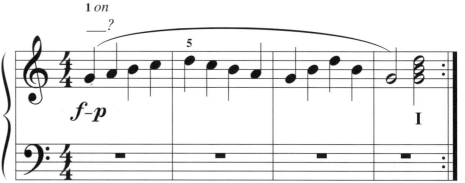

1 on ___ ?

5

f–p   **I**

FF12

New Guide Note: Low G

Bass Clef **Low G** is easy to recognize. It is written on the **bottom line** of the bass clef staff.

- Play and say: **Low G**

- Name the **intervals** in the blanks below.

Interval Study in G

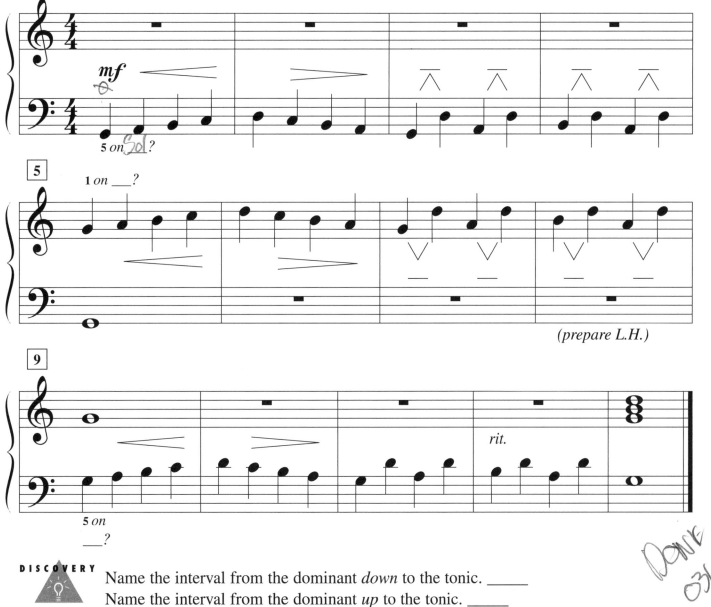

Steady, legato

mf

5 on *Sol* ?

5
1 on ___?

(prepare L.H.)

9

rit.

5 on
___?

DISCOVERY

Name the interval from the dominant *down* to the tonic. _____
Name the interval from the dominant *up* to the tonic. _____

Technique p. 56

Theory p. 59

A *musette* is a lively piece
imitating the sound of a bagpipe.

Musette

G Pentascale

Johann Sebastian Bach
(1685–1750, Germany)
arranged

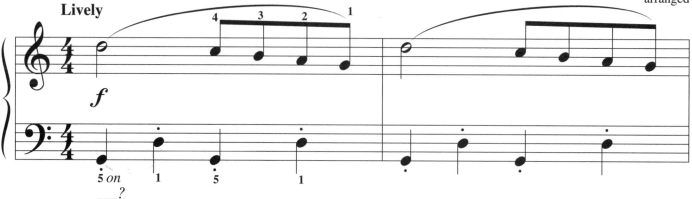

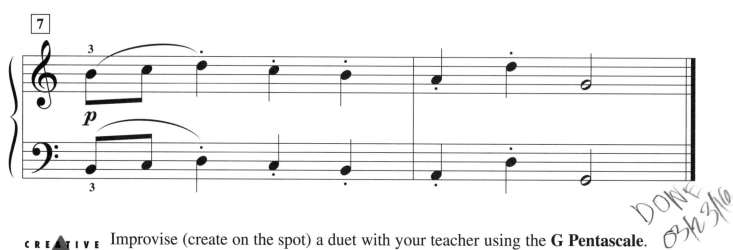

CREATIVE Improvise (create on the spot) a duet with your teacher using the **G Pentascale**.
- Your teacher will play only L.H. **tonic** and **dominant** notes as in *measures 1 and 2*.
- You create a R.H. melody above using the notes of the G Pentascale.

FF120

Review: The *natural* cancels a flat or sharp.

The **B-flat** to **B-natural** in this piece gives a "bluesy" sound.

• Play:

Hard-Drivin' Blues

G Pentascale

Driving beat

5 *on* ___?
3 *on* ___?
1 *on* ___?

f

L.H. pattern

1 *on* ___?
5 *on* ___?

DISCOVERY Which step of the **G Pentascale** is flatted in this blues piece?

scale step   1   2   3   4   5   *(circle)*

The V⁷ Chord in the Key of G

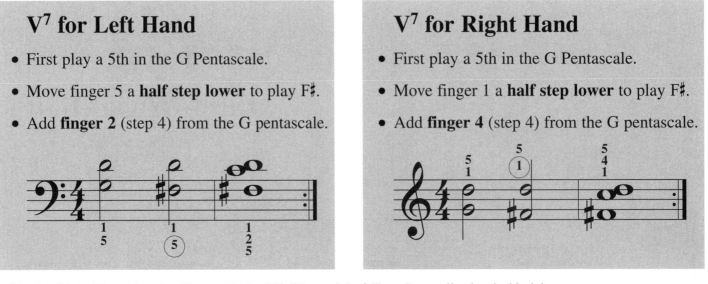

V⁷ for Left Hand

- First play a 5th in the G Pentascale.

- Move finger 5 a **half step lower** to play F♯.

- Add **finger 2** (step 4) from the G pentascale.

V⁷ for Right Hand

- First play a 5th in the G Pentascale.

- Move finger 1 a **half step lower** to play F♯.

- Add **finger 4** (step 4) from the G pentascale.

Teacher Note: The student should move the hand "in" (toward the fallboard) to easily play the black key.

tempo — means the speed of the music

- First practice at a s-l-o-w tempo.
  Listen for steady rhythm and crisp *staccatos*.

- Gradually work up to a fast tempo.

Toccatina*

Name the pentascale. _____

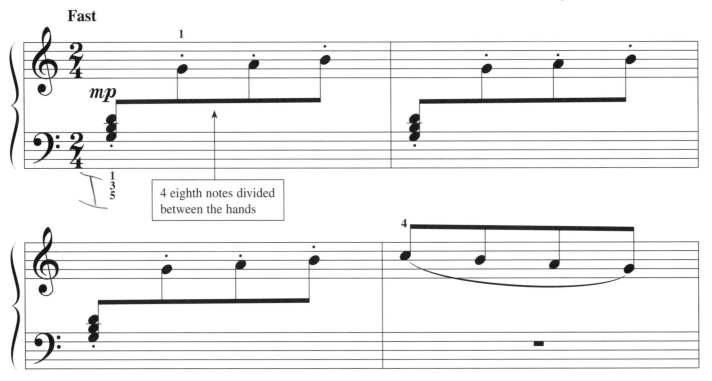

4 eighth notes divided between the hands

*A *toccatina* is a short, flashy piece played at a fast tempo. (The *toccatina* is related to the *toccata*, which is a large piece of the same character).

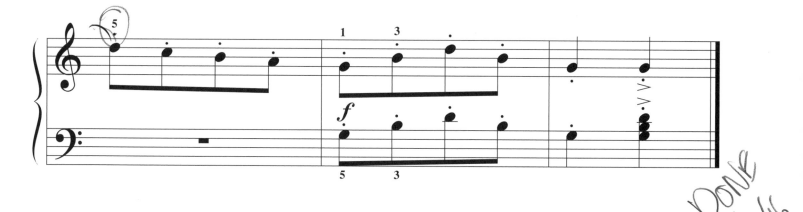

DISCOVERY Play a **G pentascale** up and down s-l-o-w-l-y with your R.H.
Harmonize *each* note by playing a **I** or **V⁷ chord** with your L.H.
Listen and let your ears guide you.

Hint: Practice these two "tricky spots" below playing hands together.

- 3rd finger cross-over at *measures 4–5.*
- R.H. finger change at *measure 9.*

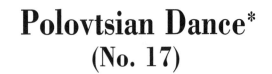

Polovtsian Dance*
(No. 17)

Alexander Borodin
(1833-1887, Russia)
arranged

Rather slow tempo

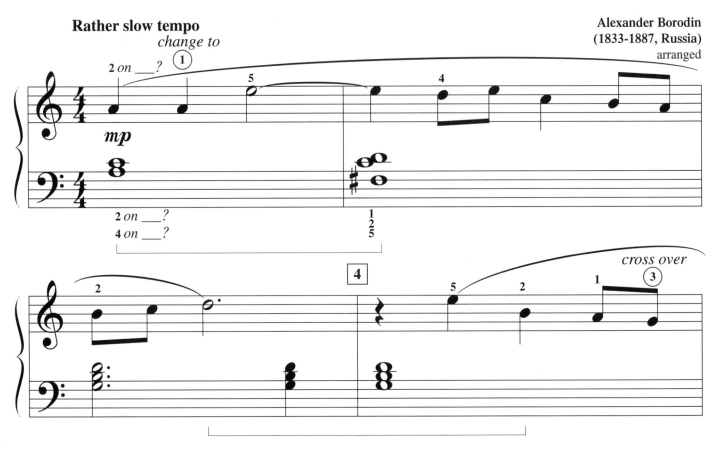

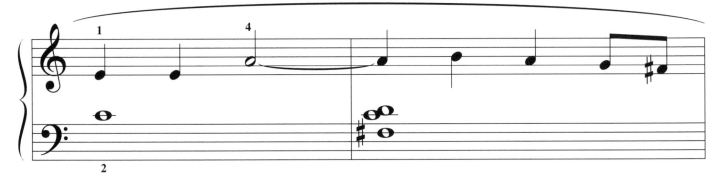

*Polovtsian - pronounced Pol-o-VETZ-ian.

Teacher Duet: (Student plays *1 octave higher*)

FF12

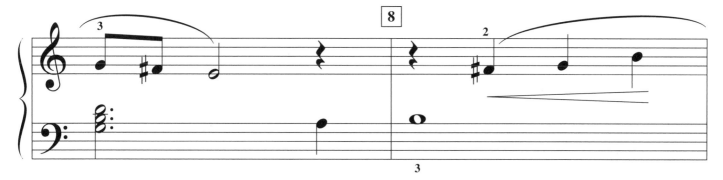

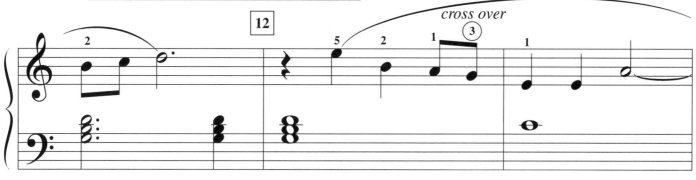

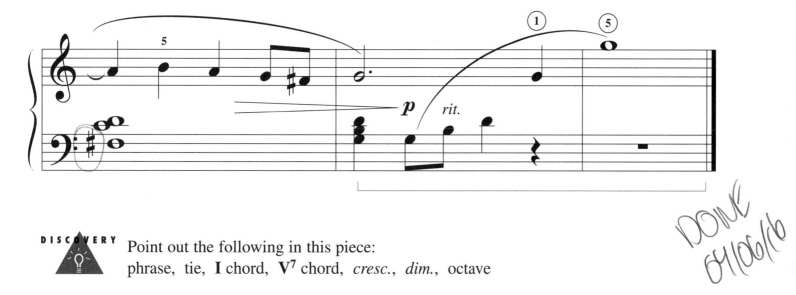

 DISCOVERY Point out the following in this piece:
phrase, tie, **I** chord, **V**^{7} chord, *cresc.*, *dim.*, octave

DONE
04/06/16

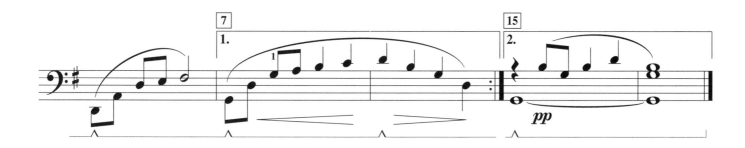

DICTIONARY OF MUSICAL TERMS

DYNAMIC MARKS

p	*mp*	*mf*	*f*
piano	*mezzo piano*	*mezzo forte*	*forte*
soft	moderately soft	moderately loud	loud

crescendo (cresc.)
Play gradually louder.

diminuendo (dim.) or decrescendo (decresc.)
Play gradually softer.

SIGN	TERM	DEFINITION
	accent mark	Play this note louder. (See p. 5)
	bar line	A line which divides the music into measures. (See p. 11)
	bass clef	The bass clef is used to show lower notes and is usually on the bottom staff. It is also called the F clef because the two dots point out the F line. (See pp. 14, 19)
	blocked chord	The notes of a chord played together. (See p. 78)
	broken chord	The notes of a chord played separately. (See p. 78)
	C pentascale	Five notes stepping up from C: C-D-E-F-G. C is the tonic. G is the dominant. (See p. 76)
	chord	Three or more notes sounding together. (See p. 78)
	I ("one") chord	Three notes built up in 3rds from the tonic note. (See p. 78)
	V^7 ("five-seven")	A four-note chord built up in 3rds from the dominant note (step 5 of the scale), often played with only three notes. (See pp. 82, 90)
	damper pedal	The right pedal, which sustains the sound. (See p. 18)
	dominant	The fifth note of the scale. (See p. 76)
	dotted half note	Three counts or beats. (See p. 27)
	double bar line	A thin, then thick bar line indicating the end of a piece. (See p. 11)
	dynamics	The "louds and softs" of music. See dynamic marks above. (See p. 70)
	eighth notes	Two eighth notes equal one quarter note. (See p. 36)
	fermata	Hold this note longer. (See Performance Book p. 32)
	1st and 2nd endings	Play the 1st ending and take the repeat, then take the 2nd ending, skipping over the 1st ending. (See p. 64)
	flat	A flat lowers a note one half step. (See p. 72)
	fifth (5th)	The interval of a 5th spans five letter names. (Ex. C up to G, or A down to D) Line-(skip-a-line)-line, or space-(skip-a-space)-space. (See pp. 60, 64)
	form	The overall structure of a piece. (See pp. 66, 80)
	fourth (4th)	The interval of a 4th spans four letter names. (Ex. C up to F, or A down to E) Line-(skip-a-line)-space, or space-(skip-a-space)-line. (See pp. 60, 61)
	G pentascale	Five notes stepping up from G: G-A-B-C-D. G is the tonic. D is the dominant. (See pp. 86, 87)
	grand staff	Two staves connected by a bar and brace, used for keyboard music. (See p. 14)
	Guide Notes	A set of memorized notes used to build reading skill. All notes of the Grand Staff may be found by reading up or down from Guide Notes. (See p. 87)
	half note	Two counts or beats (one-half the value of a whole note). (See pp. 10, 36)
	half rest	Two counts of silence. (Sits on line 3 of the staff.) (See p. 52)
	half step	The distance from one key to the very closest key on the keyboard. (Ex. D-E♭ or E-F) (See p. 68)
	harmony	Notes or chords played with the melody. (See p. 82)

FF120

SIGN	TERM	DEFINITION
	imitation	The immediate repetition of a musical idea played by the other hand. (See pp. 57, 58)
	interval	The distance between two musical tones or keys on the keyboard. (Ex. 2nd, 3rd, 4th, 5th) (See pp. 8, 42, 60, 61, 64)
	legato	Smooth, connected. (See p. 24)
	measure	Music is divided into groups of beats called measures. Each measure has an equal number of beats. (See p. 11)
	melody	The tune. (See pp. 44, 82)
	minuet	A stately dance in ¾ time. (See p. 27)
	musette	A lively piece imitating the sound of a bagpipe. (See p. 88)
	**natural**	A natural cancels a sharp or a flat (always a white key). (See pp. 74, 89)
	octave	The interval which spans 8 letter names. (Ex. C to C) (See p. 42)
8ᵛᵃ	**ottava**	Play one octave higher (or lower) than written. (See p. 56)
	pedal mark	Shows the down-up motion of the damper pedal. (See p. 18)
	phrase	A musical sentence. A phrase is often shown by a slur, also called a phrase mark. (See p. 38)
	pick-up note, upbeat	The note(s) of an incomplete opening measure. (See p. 40)
	pitch	The highness or lowness of a tone (sound). (See p. 7)
	promenade	A march of the guests at the opening of an important event. (See p. 61)
	quarter note	One count or beat. (One-quarter the value of a whole note.) (See pp. 10, 36)
	quarter rest	One beat of silence. (See p. 32)
	repeated note	A note on the same line or space as the preceding note. (See p. 16)
	retrograde	A musical idea played backwards. (See p. 53)
rit.	**ritardando**	Gradually slowing down. (See p. 77)
	second (2nd) (step)	The interval that spans two letter names. (Ex. C up to D, or F down to E) On the staff: line-to-the-next-space or space-to-the-next-line. (See pp. 8, 11, 13, 30)
♯	**sharp**	A sharp raises a note one half step. (See p. 68)
	slur	A curved line that indicates legato playing. (See p. 24)
	staccato	Detached, disconnected. (See p. 46)
	staff	The five lines and four spaces on which notes are written. (See p. 14)
	tempo	The speed of the music. (See p. 90)
	theme	A melody made of several phrases. (See p. 44)
	third (3rd) (skip)	The interval that spans three letter names. (Ex. C up to E, or F down to D) On the staff: line-to-the-next-line or space-to-the-next-space. (See pp. 8, 11, 13, 30)
	tie	A curved line that connects two notes on the same line or space. Hold for the total counts of both notes. (See p. 34)
²⁄₄ ³⁄₄ ⁴⁄₄	**time signature**	Two numbers at the beginning of a piece (one above the other). The top number indicates the number of beats per measure; the bottom number indicates the note receiving one beat. (See pp. 15, 46)
	tonic	The first note of the scale. (See pp. 76, 86)
𝄞	**treble clef**	The treble clef is used to show higher notes and is usually on the top staff. It is also called the G clef because the treble clef circles around the G line. (See pp. 14, 17)
	variation	An alteration of the theme: different notes, rhythm, or dynamics, etc. (See Performance Book p. 11)
	waltz	A dance piece in ¾ time. (See p. 49)
𝅝	**whole note**	Four counts or beats. (See pp. 10, 36)
	**whole rest**	Four beats of silence, or silence for any whole measure. (Hangs below line 4.) (See p. 52)

Certificate of Achievement

Congratulations to:

ALIREZA GHIRIAN

You have completed BOOK 1 of
ACCELERATED PIANO ADVENTURES®
for the Older Beginner
and are now ready for

BOOK 2 ACCELERATED PIANO ADVENTURES®
for the Older Beginner

Teacher: _Sarah Mohman_   Date: _April 6, 2016_